MYTHS OF
MARKETING

BANISH THE MISCONCEPTIONS
AND BECOME A GREAT MARKETER

Grant Leboff

KoganPage

First published in Great Britain and the United States in 2020 by Kogan Page Limited

2nd Floor, 45 Gee Street	122 W 27th St, 10th Floor	4737/23 Ansari Road
London	New York, NY 10001	Daryaganj
EC1V 3RS	USA	New Delhi 110002
United Kingdom		India

www.koganpage.com

ISBNs

Hardback	978 0 7494 9848 1
Paperback	978 0 7494 8391 3
eBook	978 0 7494 8392 0

British Library Cataloguing-in-Publication Data

A CIP record for this book is available from the British Library.

Library of Congress Cataloging-in-Publication Data

Names: Leboff, Grant, author.
Title: Myths of marketing : banish the misconceptions and become a great marketer / Grant Leboff.
Description: 1st Edition. | New York : Kogan Page, 2020. | Includes bibliographical references and index. |
Identifiers: LCCN 2019044258 (print) | LCCN 2019044259 (ebook) | ISBN 9780749498481 (hardback) | ISBN 9780749483913 (paperback) | ISBN 9780749483920 (ebook)
Subjects: LCSH: Marketing.
Classification: LCC HF5415 .L3617 2020 (print) | LCC HF5415 (ebook) | DDC 658.8–dc23

Typeset by Integra Software Services, Pondicherry
Print production managed by Jellyfish
Printed and bound by CPI Group (UK) Ltd, Croydon CR0 4YY

CONTENTS

PREFACE

From a historical perspective we can trace where we are today back to the fall of the Berlin Wall. It was after this that Eastern European markets began opening up to trade [1]. This, alongside the continuing growth of the Asian economies meant that business started to become a truly global affair [2].

High-tech innovation then made this even more of a reality. Digital technology enabled an increasing number of entrepreneurs to start enterprises with merely a computer and a mobile phone. With such a low barrier to market there were more companies competing for business than ever before [3]. Meanwhile, technological innovation resulted in consumers going online and purchasing products from all over the world, in the comfort of their own homes.

These developments, together with the invention of the World Wide Web, the subsequent creation of social platforms and the ubiquitous adoption of smart phones, have led us to where we are today.

We have now reached a point where, for the first time in history, organizations, businesses and individuals have their own media channels. Today, there is more information, communication and content competing for our attention than ever.

This means that we are living in a world with tremendous opportunities. Never before has it been so easy to start a business or to access knowledge and ideas from around the world. Not at any time in history have individuals, organizations or businesses had the ability to communicate on such a large scale with tools that are readily available to all.

On the other hand, there has never been more competition for customers' share of wallet and share of mind. Consumers have nearly infinite choice about where to spend their money, as businesses compete for our attention.

As a result, marketing is a discipline that is being practised by more people than ever. Quite apart from the many dedicated marketing professionals who are working across the globe, business leaders, c-suite executives, business owners and individuals are all trying to get the most out of the media channels at their disposal, and for that, an understanding of marketing is a prerequisite for success.

This requirement for a burgeoning number of individuals to participate in marketing activities means that it is becoming a little like sports management, whereby every armchair supporter has an opinion, which they believe is equally as valid as professionals who have spent years working in the game.

As well as this, the specialisms that have developed due to digital technology, such as the building of websites, organic search engine optimization (SEO), pay per click (PPC) and social media advertising have also led more people to generically call themselves marketing experts, when in reality, they have proficiency in the execution of a particular marketing tactic.

All this has culminated in the dissemination of many myths, fictions and untruths about marketing that are now taken as valid when, in fact, they are nothing of the sort. In this climate, what we need are genuine answers to questions such as:

- How has digital technology really impacted the nature of communications?
- What is the real difference between sales and marketing?
- Why is word of mouth not just happenchance but a bona fide marketing channel?

Myths of Marketing is written to cut through the misinformation and provide reasoned and researched answers to some of today's most important questions.

From understanding that marketing is not contained in a single department, to recognizing how different price perceptions can affect your value proposition and understanding the importance of market positioning, *Myths of Marketing* will arm you with the insights you need in order to be effective.

If you are ready to banish the misconceptions and become a great marketer, then *Myths of Marketing* might just be the book for you.

Notes

1 Halligan, L (2014) Fall of the Berlin Wall opened up a world of opportunity, *Daily Telegraph*, 08 November [online] www.telegraph. co.uk/finance/comment/11218533/Fall-of-the-Berlin-Wall-opened-a-world-of-opportunity.html (archived at https://perma.cc/ 57JW-H8DV) [accessed 13 June 2019]

2 Ortiz-Ospina, E, Beltekian, D and Roser, M (2014) Trade and globalization, *Our World In Data* [online] ourworldindata.org/ trade-and-globalization (archived at https://perma.cc/YZ4E-374A) [accessed 13 June 2019]

3 Bounds, A (2017) Number of UK start-ups rises to new record, *Financial Times*, 12 October [online] www.ft.com/content/cb56d86c-88d6-11e7-afd2-74b8ecd34d3b (archived at https://perma.cc/ TBV8-5X7S) [accessed 13 June 2019]

MARKETING COMMUNICATIONS HAVEN'T FUNDAMENTALLY CHANGED

Before the proliferation of digital technology, the overwhelming majority of the information we obtained came from traditional media companies. We received the news from broadcasters on radio and television or in magazines and newspapers. We read books and trade magazines from publishers, listened to music from record companies and watched TV programmes and films, produced and distributed by studios. It was these entities that had the sole means of distribution and could reach a wider audience.

A number of developments then changed this paradigm. By 1989, some of the largest commercial email services in the world such as MCI Mail, Ontyme, Telemail and CompuServe had connected their respective email systems to the internet, thus connecting them with each other for the first time, and marking 'the start of commercial Internet services in the United States' [1]. This was followed by British scientist Tim Berners-Lee's invention of the World Wide Web, while working at CERN. By December of 1990 Berners-Lee had built all the tools needed for a working World Wide Web [2]. Then, in April 1993 CERN put the World Wide Web software in the public domain, making it available on a royalty-free basis. This open licence maximized dissemination and, as stated on the CERN website, it was these actions that 'allowed the web to flourish' [3].

As the web developed, social media emerged. Six Degrees, created by Andrew Weinreich in May 1996 and launched the following year, is widely considered to have been the very first social networking site. It 'combined popular features such as profiles, friends lists and school affiliations in one service' [4]. These phenomena, together with the increasing adoption of smart phones in the first decade of the 2000s, changed the nature of communications.

Today, everyone owns media channels. Companies such as the BBC, Comcast, CBS Corporation and Viacom are still broadcasting as they always did. In fact, by utilizing the web, streaming services and apps, many of the world's largest media companies have a bigger output than ever before. While these enterprises have expanded their offerings, the shift is that now businesses and organizations also own media.

A media channel is essentially a distribution medium for reaching an audience. Entities such as a website, Facebook page, LinkedIn profile, YouTube channel or Instagram account should be treated as media channels, as they provide a company with the ability to reach an audience. What makes any of these compelling is the content an organization posts on these platforms.

Marketing Communications (marcom) used to be the craft of interrupting someone else's audience. A business would decide on a market it would like to target, and then pay the entity that had that audience's attention. For example, a training provider wanting to reach HR professionals may have decided to advertise in an HR magazine dedicated to that profession.

Radio, TV, cinema, billboards, journals, newspapers and magazines were used to interrupt people in the same way. Similarly, direct mail enabled organizations to obtain eyeballs, using the postal system, by purchasing stamps. Telemarketing utilized the telephone network through call charges. Of course, there are times when paying to interrupt an audience will remain part of a marcom strategy. If it is effective, there is no reason why it should not be a component.

However, digital now dominates every facet of our lives and needs to be right at the core of any marcom strategy. Operating these channels relies less on traditional marcom disciplines and more on practices associated with the media. Today, an organization can invest in building a brilliant website, put together an amazing Facebook page or create the most marvellous YouTube channel but, unlike in traditional marcom, there will be no immediate audience. In other words, businesses now need to build an audience and retain it. This is a traditional media discipline, not a marketing one.

If media channels are only as good as the content they disseminate, then companies now have to create compelling material that is pertinent to their business, while ensuring it is relevant to their audience. Of course, traditionalists will point to the fact that creating content was always the job of marcom. After all, brochures, guides, leaflets, adverts, commercials, direct mail pieces, and the many other types of materials that companies produced, are all content.

However, there is a fundamental difference. This content was designed to garner the attention of an existing audience for a few seconds. A lot of the communications were transactional in nature, encouraging an immediate response from a prospect. As a business was paying the broadcaster or publisher for a moment in time, these communications were sporadic and normally based around a campaign a company was running. For example, even the most vociferous of TV advertisers may only put out a few adverts per year.

Just as broadcasters must put out new programmes daily to ensure their media channels remain interesting, vibrant and enticing, organizations also need to generate a constant stream of fresh content. This material cannot be merely transactional, simply espousing the virtues of a business. There is a limit to how many times an individual would visit a company's different media channels if all they did was state the greatness of the enterprise. This approach is unlikely to build an audience and certainly won't retain it, as no one would ever come back. Instead the content should provide the specific audience with value, regardless of whether a transaction will take place in the immediate future.

For example, a recruitment business may put out material about how to attract staff, great interview techniques and questions, how to retain staff as well as a benchmarking table to provide regional businesses with a rough guide to wages within their specific locality. All of this material is relevant as it directly relates to recruitment. Yet a business owner or HR department would not need to be contemplating using a recruitment company in order to find this content useful. They may subscribe to a newsletter, sign up for alerts or choose to regularly visit the company's website as it becomes a useful source of information.

If this business owner or HR department ever does need to use the services of a recruitment company, it is probable that this particular business will receive the enquiry. They may well explore other recruitments agencies and this organization cannot guarantee it will receive work, but having consistent engagement with the recruitment firm makes it likely it would be in their buying set. This is what marcom should achieve; that is, when someone in a company's target market is looking for its products or services, it receives the enquiry.

As stated earlier in the chapter, in previous times a company's main marketing activities would involve paying to interrupt an audience built by a media organization around its magazine, radio programme or TV show etc. In a world where businesses possess their own channels they, like the media companies, need to build their own audience and retain it. There are two other changes in the digital age that make this approach essential.

First, it is not just media companies and businesses that own their own media channels. Billions of individuals are also posting content on platforms such as Facebook, Instagram, LinkedIn, Twitter and YouTube. The result is that we now live in a world of information overload. In essence, every individual and organization is now a media entity.

Everything in life has a cause and effect. The direct effect of inhabiting a world where there is an abundance of information is that we now reside in a world of scarcity of attention. 'Attention' is the resource that every business requires in order to be successful. Today, it is the companies with your attention that 'win'.

For example, one of the aspects that makes Amazon so formidable is that it is not merely an e-commerce platform but a product search engine. People use Amazon to understand the choice and price variations in a particular product category. Once it has a customer's attention at the beginning of the buying journey, with one click to purchase and next-day delivery, it will receive a good percentage of the business.

Not only do digital platforms work like media channels, whereby a company is required to build an audience and retain it, but there is a commercial imperative in doing so. In a world where attention is scarce, it is the companies with their audiences' attention that will 'win'. Companies were once valuable because of 'what' they did; businesses today are valuable because of the attention they have.

This brings us to the second change. Inhabiting a world where everyone owns media channels has changed the dynamic of how information is distributed. Traditionally, in broadcast, a TV show or radio programme would receive as many listeners or viewers as tuned in or recorded the episode at a particular time. While occasionally people would lend each other video tapes of programmes, offices were not full of individuals swapping videos every day. Of course, in the world of publishing, people would share books and magazines. It is estimated that the average newspaper is read by three more people than purchase it [5]. So, social sharing has always taken place.

The difference is that in the digital world, social sharing doesn't just take place, it is the currency of media. It is the primary way that information is discovered online, and this has severe implications for marcom. In traditional communications, there were fundamentally two different aspects: the audience comprised the people a business wanted to reach; the channel was the mechanism used to get to the audience. So, as in our previous example, HR professionals may be the audience and an HR magazine would be the channel used to reach this target market.

In the digital age where everyone has a channel, and consequently social sharing plays such a pivotal role in the way information is discovered, the audience is no longer merely the people whom a business wants to reach. They also become a significant channel in their own right. They are now a company's best marketers and a key purchase influencer: as the proverb states, 'birds of a feather flock together'. Accountants know accountants, lawyers know lawyers, followers of a particular sports team are likely to know other followers. In a digital environment, an engaged audience can be an excellent channel for reaching other people of a similar type.

When media companies controlled the distribution of information, marcom was the discipline of interrupting someone else's audience. Today, when all businesses and organizations own their own media channels, marcom is not merely about interrupting an audience but also building one and then ensuring it is retained. In a world where attention is becoming a progressively scarce resource and information is increasingly being disseminated via social sharing, this approach is not simply how digital works, but it also makes commercial sense. This being the case, marketing communications has changed in a fundamental way.

Notes

1 Internet history of 1980s, *Computer History* [online] www.computerhistory.org/internethistory/1980s/ (archived at https://perma.cc/4DFT-6AD4) [accessed 1 February 2018]

2 Pre-W3C web and internet background, *W3C* [online] www.w3.org/2004/Talks/w3c10-HowItAllStarted/?n=15 (archived at https://perma.cc/QTF5-CX4S) [accessed 6 August 2019]

3 The birth of the web, *CERN* [online] home.cern/topics/birth-web (archived at https://perma.cc/2RS8-6NEW) [accessed 6 August 2019]

4 Then and now: a history of social networking sites, *CBS* [online] www.cbsnews.com/pictures/then-and-now-a-history-of-social-networking-sites/2/ (archived at https://perma.cc/6XG9-V6WP) [accessed 1 January 2018]

5 Greenslade, R (2010) Look how many newspapers are still sold every day in the UK, *Guardian*, 14 December [online] www.theguardian.com/media/greenslade/2010/dec/14/newspapers-abcs (archived at https://perma.cc/62TB-ZDQB) [accessed 1 January 2018]

MYTH
2

MARKETING IS JUST COMMUNICATIONS

There is no one agreed definition of marketing. The American Marketing Association states that 'Marketing is the activity, set of institutions and processes for creating, communicating, delivering and exchanging offerings that have value for customers, clients, partners and society at large' [1].

The UK's Chartered Institute of Marketing asserts that 'Marketing is the management process responsible for identifying, anticipating and satisfying customer requirements profitably' [2]. Alternatively, Philip Kotler, widely seen as one of the world's leading marketing thinkers [3], says that 'Marketing is the science and art of exploring, creating, and delivering value to satisfy the needs of a target market at a profit' [4].

Although these definitions vary, they share a lot of commonalities. I would define marketing as the process of determining, communicating and delivering value in order to obtain and retain customers. This definition fits well with Peter Drucker, one of the most influential thinkers on business management, and his explanation of what marketing should accomplish, that is 'to create, keep and satisfy the customer' [5].

David Packard, co-founder of Hewlett Packard, famously said, 'Marketing is too important to be left to the marketing department' [6].

This being the case, the areas that were most often left to marketing were the promotional activities and the tactical deliverables such as brochures, direct mails and adverts. That is, the communications. Meanwhile, the strategic elements of marketing were carried out elsewhere and perhaps, therefore, were not perceived as marketing at all.

Peter Drucker agrees, stating that marketing encompassed the entire business, that 'it is the whole business seen from the point of view of its final result, that is from the customer's point of view. Concern and responsibility for marketing, therefore, permeate all areas of the enterprise' [7].

While communication is a key component in marketing, there are other considerations. The different factors that must be taken into account are often referred to as 'the marketing mix', a term first used in 1953 by Neil Borden, a Harvard professor, when addressing the American Marketing Association [8].

The most famous model of the 'marketing mix' is the '4 Ps' created in 1960 by E. Jerome McCarthy [9]. It provides a foundation for the different considerations on which marketing should focus. These are:

Product – this is the offering that the customer will receive. It can be made up of one or many components including a product, service, experience or a combination of all of these.

Place – this is the medium or mediums by which a customer can access the offer.

Price – refers to the cost for the customer. This is not just the amount charged but the time and effort that a customer may need to exert through the purchase, the expenditure that might be required to implement the solution, and any other expenses that may be associated with the acquisition.

Promotion – the mechanisms employed to ensure potential customers are aware of the offering, to educate them as to why they would want to invest in the proposition and to make it as enticing as possible.

While the '4 Ps' model, as a framework, is still appropriate many decades after it was first conceived, the language used does not resonate in a 21st-century world. It should be updated. The model I propose is the acronym CAVE, which is as follows:

Communication. It could be argued that by definition, all marcom is promotional. After all, organizations only communicate in order to encourage sales somewhere down the line. However, in a world where enterprises own media channels, much of the content they produce should be created to provide value to their audience, rather than being promotional in the conventional sense.

This would not have been the case in 1960. Most communications at that time would have been purely promotional and therefore the word 'promotion' as a catch-all term would have been more applicable. Of course, there will be times today when communications are 'promotional' in the purest sense.

When organizations are running their own media channels, there needs to be a greater richness and depth to their communications. The word 'promotion' does not encapsulate this reality. Communications need to be considered in their broadest terms. Companies will then use a variety of mechanisms within this discipline to achieve their desired outcomes.

Access. Before a world of e-commerce, applications and software, the purchase of products and services normally required some physical contact with a supplier. There were definite 'places' where these interactions would occur and the term 'place' was completely appropriate.

Today in an omni-channel world, where it is often the case that direct interaction is not required for a purchase to occur, thinking in terms of 'place' can seem a little restricting. Considering an offering in terms of 'access' and the different opportunities that can be created for interactions, communications and touch-points, with prospects and customers, is more appropriate in the digital era.

Value. Price is normally the direct compensation given to one entity by another in return for the receipt of products or services. Price is quite a one-dimensional concept as there are many other factors that may need considering. For example, there is the time and effort that needs to be exerted into making a particular purchase. There is the context in which the purchase occurs. There is the expense of implementing a solution and the cost of ownership and maintenance. There are also personal reputations that will be contemplated, and other risks that might be deemed a liability in making the acquisition. All of these come at a cost and will be taken into account.

Ultimately, all purchases are a value exchange. An individual, or company, will need to feel that what they are getting is greater or similar in value to what they are being asked to concede. Engagement with a business, via its website or social media channels, may not require any monetary compensation from a prospect, but they will have to give time, attention and effort. Therefore, a 'value exchange' is always taking place even when an offering appears, on the surface, to be free.

Experience. In a world of abundance, where customers have a multitude of choices, and consequently so many offerings have been commoditized, differentiation is often not delivered by 'what' a company does – 'the product' – but by 'how' it is done – the experience.

For example, most accountants deliver similar services such as auditing, tax advice, financial planning, payroll and business consultation amongst many others. In terms of 'what' they do, it is almost impossible for any of them to differentiate themselves. However, while one accountancy practice might focus on corporate companies, another may target owner/managers and entrepreneurs. Consequently, the firm working with corporates may be a lot more formal in its style of delivery and be used to conversations that are quite technical as they will be mainly working with finance directors who are well versed in the specific terminology. Meanwhile, the practice serving entrepreneurs may be a lot more informal and take great pride in explaining concepts in an easy-to-understand manner. While 'what' these firms deliver, in terms of services, will be similar, 'how' they work with clients will be quite different.

This focus on experience is magnified in a post-industrial era where an increasing number of consumers, and therefore consumer offerings, are no longer concerned with 'basic needs', according to Maslow's hierarchy, but are more focused on psychological needs and those of self-fulfilment [10]. As products have become commodities, basic offerings are often very similar and available at almost any price. Low-cost providers in categories such as fashion, air travel and electronics often mean that consumers are no longer choosing 'whether' they can afford to purchase but rather are discerning about 'what' they buy.

Furthermore, media relies on personalities and narrative. In an era where everyone owns a media channel, this often makes it easier to share experiences rather than physical products. Whereas taking a picture of a new car and posting it to friends might be construed as showing off, sharing experiences such as attending a sporting event, a pop concert, or taking a picture from the top of the Eiffel Tower will be perceived as interesting.

As we enter the 'experience economy' it is more helpful for an organization to think of its offering in terms of an 'experience' instead of a product or service. Experiences are more three dimensional and encapsulate all emotions, interactions, participation and deliverables that may involve a customer in their dealings with an enterprise. Experience is a more appropriate word than product in the 21st-century economy.

Since the establishment of the '4 Ps' in 1960 there have been attempts to add to them. For example, in order to reflect the service economy, People, Process and Physical Evidence are three more Ps that were added by Bernard H Booms and Mary J Bitner to make up their proposed 7 Ps of Marketing [11]. These additions seem to me unnecessary. As I proposed at the beginning of this chapter, marketing is the process of determining, communicating and delivering value in order to obtain and retain customers. In other words, it is a completely customer-focused discipline. While an organization will require the right people and processes in order to deliver an excellent service, internally this is an operational issue, not a marketing one.

People, Process and Physical Evidence from a marketing perspective are already covered in our CAVE acronym. People and Process, from a customer perspective, are part of the 'Experience' that an organization creates. Meanwhile, being able to provide customers with Physical Evidence as to the effectiveness of an offering is part of 'Communication' in educating the customer and making the offer attractive.

Similarly, in retail, proposed additions have included 'Personnel' and 'Presentation', in what is known as the '6 Ps of Retailing' [12]. Again, I would argue that Personnel and Presentation, from a customer perspective, are part of the 'Experience' covered in the CAVE acronym.

Once there is an understanding that marketing is not simply communications, then other disciplines associated with marketing can be better understood. Market segmentation involves dividing a large market into smaller groups based on common characteristics. Pertinent ways to segment a market will change based on the offering. Some common ways to segment markets are:

Geographic – where location or the natural features or characteristics of a region are relevant.

Psychographic – considers personality traits, values, attitudes, interests, and lifestyles of a particular group.

Demographic – includes age, race, religion, gender, family size, ethnicity, income, and education.

Behavioural – focuses on the distinct actions users have taken, for example buying behaviour such as patterns of buying as well as items, categories and brands purchased. Usage includes actions such as how many times a customer has accessed an offer, when it is used, how it is used, the context in which it is used etc.

Market segmentation is important because the more homogeneous a group, the easier it will be to 'determine, communicate and deliver value to them' and therefore obtain and retain them as customers.

Determining value for a particular group is a key part of marketing. This could result in any number of activities. It could include a marketing team participating in the creation of a new product or service, tailoring an offering or experience in order to appeal to a target market, or deciding the best way to position the offering in order to attract customers. Of course, these are just a few of the many ways marketing could be involved in determining value.

To ensure that those people undertaking marketing truly understand their customers so that they can deliver value, market research and studies will often be undertaken. Fundamentally, marketing requires people to have a comprehensive understanding of their target market and how the challenges, problems, hopes, ambitions, goals and aspirations of these people relate to the offerings that the organization provides.

Ultimately, marketing necessitates thinking about the enterprise from the point of view of the customer and their requirements. Communication is a part of this, but it is so much more.

Notes

1 AMA, American Marketing Association (2013) Definition of Marketing /07 [online] www.ama.org/AboutAMA/Pages/Definition-of-Marketing.aspx (archived at https://perma.cc/TY98-6NGA) [accessed 11 March 2018]

2 CIM, Chartered Institute of Marketing (2015) Marketing and the 7Ps: A brief summary of marketing and how it works [online] www.cim.co.uk/media/4772/7ps.pdf (archived at https://perma.cc/XS4T-ZQTG) [accessed 07 March 2018]

3 Kaul, V (2012) Beyond advertising: Philip Kotler remains one of the most influential marketing thinkers. *The Economic Times* 29 February [online] economictimes.indiatimes.com/magazines/brand-equity/beyond-advertising-philip-kotler-remains-one-of-the-most-influential-marketing-thinkers/articleshow/12077931.cms (archived at https://perma.cc/8M9S-RSR8) [accessed 07 March 2018]

4 Kotler, P (nd) Dr Philip Kotler answers your questions on marketing, *Kotler Marketing Group* [online] www.kotlermarketing.com/phil_questions.shtml (archived at https://perma.cc/N85N-HVSC) [accessed 07 March 2018]

5 Drucker, P F (1955) *The Practice of Management,* Routledge, London

6 Trout, J (2006) Peter Drucker on marketing, *Forbes.com*, 03 July [online] www.forbes.com/2006/06/30/jack-trout-on-marketing-cx_jt_0703drucker.html#19fbc8a6555c (archived at https://perma.cc/VJ8R-26VM) [accessed 07 March 2018]

7 Groucutt, J, Leadley, P and Forsyth, P (2004) *Marketing: Essential principles, new realities,* Kogan Page, London

8 Dorling Kindersley (2014) *The Business Book*, Dorling Kindersley, London

9 Oxford Reference (nd) E Jerome McCarthy [online] www.oxfordreference.com/view/10.1093/oi/authority.20110803100143321 (archived at https://perma.cc/S7M5-WTLS) [accessed 08 March 2018]

10 Libert, B (2014) Finance: why businesses should serve consumers' 'higher needs', *Wharton* [online] knowledge.wharton.upenn.edu/article/why-businesses-should-serve-consumers-higher-needs/ (archived at https://perma.cc/HFW6-UD7Z) [accessed 28 March 2018]

11 Booms, B H and Bitner, M J (1981) Marketing strategies and organizational structures for service firms, in *Marketing of Services*, ed J Donnelly and W R George, American Marketing Association, Chicago

12 Barron, M (2014) 6 P's of retailing, *Insights 2 Marketing*, 13 December [online] insights2marketing.wordpress.com/retailing/6p/ (archived at https://perma.cc/2DFN-3UNY) [accessed 08 March 2018]

SALES AND MARKETING ARE BASICALLY THE SAME

In Myth 2 we saw that marketing is 'the process of determining, communicating and delivering value in order to obtain and retain customers'. If selling is the act of inducing someone to buy [1], then it is easy to recognize that both salespeople and marketers have a common objective: to obtain customers. Perhaps it is this common goal that leads to the confusion surrounding the differences between the two.

In Myth 2 we redefined the marketing mix using the acronym CAVE – Communication, Access, Value and Experience. When we examine sales through this prism, the contrasts between these different disciplines become clear.

Communication is the main area in which the two meet. In fact, personal selling, the use of an individual to encourage someone to buy, is one form of communication, as are advertising, direct marketing or public relations. This being the case, it is right to say that personal selling is a subset of marketing. This does not mean that those involved in sales activities do not require a unique set of skills, techniques and competencies to excel. It is a recognition that personal selling is just one way of communicating with prospects and customers.

However, it is in the nature of the communication where the difference lies. Marketing is responsible for communications from the brand or organization to the marketplace, whereas salespeople undertake person-to-person communications as representatives of the business.

There are plenty of products where marketing, or brand-to-person communications, result in sales. The whole category of Fast-Moving Consumer Goods (FMCG) is an example. The marketing of soft drinks, toothpaste or washing up liquid will lead people to purchase particular brands without any need for individual salespeople.

There are many consumer offerings which, because of their complexity, impact or cost, will require person-to-person communication. For example, a couple planning a holiday of a lifetime, at significant expense, may feel uncomfortable booking the entire trip themselves. They may want to utilize the experience of an expert who can help them tailor the holiday. In this case, the reassurance of speaking to a person makes this communication necessary for the company to 'obtain the customer'. For this couple, the marketing, that is the brand-to-person communication, could only take them so far down the purchase journey; it required a sales representative to secure the transaction.

Similarly, there are many business-to-business offerings which, because of the significant investment, complexity and impact on the organization, require person-to-person communication as part of the buying journey. For example, it is unlikely that a software platform that requires distinct customization, and which costs hundreds of thousands of dollars, would be purchased without the guidance and reassurance of some person-to-person communication. In its quest to obtain and retain customers, as part of the 'communication' aspect of marketing, the company offering this software may use personal selling as a major component to achieve results.

Salespeople are employed when individual interaction is required in order to secure transactions. This makes the attainment of transactions the sole focus of sales. Although, ultimately, the effectiveness of marketing also has to be judged on transactions, the mechanism by which customers are obtained and retained, communication, is only one of the disciplines of marketing. Therefore, the scope of its activities is far wider than sales.

It is often perceived in the business-to-business environment that marketing's job is to generate leads, while the role of sales is to convert these leads into transactions. If marketing is the process of 'determining, communicating and delivering value in order to obtain and retain customers' then by definition it must create leads. In other words, marketing activities should result in people expressing an interest and buying the offering a company provides.

However, salespeople are often charged with generating leads for themselves. Traditionally, they would employ person-to-person methods such as door knocking, telephoning, networking and attending exhibitions and events in order to establish sales opportunities. While specific companies may choose to make lead generation the sole responsibility of marketing, it is not a difference that delineates the roles in a general sense. Marketing will generate leads utilizing brand-to-person communication, whereas sales will undertake this task on a person-to-person basis.

Access is the area of the CAVE marketing mix whereby marketers must consider how and where an offering will be made available to customers. Access can have a huge effect on the perception of a product, its desirability to the target audience and its ultimate success. This is a strategic marketing discipline and not one that involves sales. Of course, in direct interactions with customers, salespeople may well uncover requirements of which the marketing department may be unaware. Organizations should have mechanisms to ensure this 'market intelligence' filters back into the company.

Today, salespeople have to think about access in ways they would not have done previously. Traditionally, salespeople would 'bash down doors'. Whether by selling door to door, making 'cold calls' or attending the right exhibitions or events – salespeople would approach prospects directly. In the digital age, with so much information at their disposal, buyers are completing much more of the purchase journey on their own, without the need for guidance. Having been empowered, they are less open to these 'cold' approaches.

Consequently, salespeople are having to ask questions traditionally explored by marketers such as 'Where do my customers learn?' 'What are the platforms, forums and associations that people might utilize at the beginning of a buyer journey?' Salespeople will often need to have a presence in these places. As many of these channels will be online and are essentially media channels, salespeople have the requirement to write blogs, create video and other materials in order to build a platform from which they can sell. While marketers have always created content, salespeople did not previously have to design their own brochures, develop adverts or run their own direct mail campaigns. Salespeople are now having to learn, at some level, disciplines that were solely the remit of marketing in years gone by.

Conversely, marketers may find the need to communicate person to person with their customers, for example via online tools such as social media. This traditionally was the domain of the salesperson. As more of the purchase journey migrates online, marketers are needing to develop more understanding of how to move a purchase forward. This in many sectors was the remit of salespeople. This overlap means that sales and marketing departments have to work much more closely together today than was once the case.

This presents itself in two particular ways. First, salespeople may well need marketing support to produce content for their online channels. Second, marketing and sales departments need to ensure they are very much aligned. Whereas in previous generations each department may have utilized very different communication channels, today they are both online. A lack of a consistent approach between the two could impair the effectiveness of both.

For instance, a customer may read some material on a salesperson's social media platform and immediately visit the company website, under marketing's remit, to learn more. If the messaging is not consistent in tone, feel and language, the result could be a confused customer who feels that they don't understand the offering and consequently looks elsewhere.

The value part of the marketing mix, and whether the offering is worth the time and money, comes under the jurisdiction of marketing. Considerations such as setting the price while factoring in the time and effort required to make a purchase, the context in which the purchase takes place, the expense involved in implementing the solution and the cost of ownership and maintenance are all strategic issues. These must be deliberated to ensure that customers perceive the offering as attractive. Salespeople can play a key role in these strategic issues in that they may have 'market intelligence' which should be fed back to the organization. They also need to have an acute understanding of what is important to a customer, and the value being offered to them, in order to be able to sell effectively. It is not the responsibility of salespeople though to determine this value – it is firmly controlled by marketing.

The final part of the marketing mix is the experience itself. This is the product or service on offer, including all the different aspects a customer will encounter. This will include the interactions that take place, any participation that is involved and the emotions that are evoked. Conventionally, determining the scope of the product or service, and what the customer should experience, was the remit of marketing and this is still the case. The difference is that today salespeople contribute to, and directly impact, the experience.

As I outlined in Myth 2, in a world of abundance, where so many offerings have been commoditized, differentiation is often not delivered by 'what' a company does, the 'product' or 'service', but by 'how' it is done, 'the experience'. As often the first *human* interaction an individual has with a business is with a salesperson, 'the experience', provided by the salesperson, will have an effect on the buyer's perception of an organization. When products or services seem similar, but the salesperson from one particular business adds real value in the questions they ask, the insight they provide and the observations they make, then this buying 'experience' may secure the deal, as well as set customer expectations.

In a product-based economy, irrespective of how great the salesperson was, the customer knew they were buying a tangible item which would not be altered by the quality of a salesperson. In an experience-based economy, the people representing the company are part of the experience. Therefore, the selling process itself can be the differentiator. While it is still the job of marketing to determine the experience, it is vital that they work closely with the sales department to ensure salespeople understand the tenets of the offering and are representing it properly in their own interactions with customers.

So, sales and marketing are different disciplines, despite sharing the same goal. But in a digital world there has been a blurring of the lines between the two. Salespeople now own media channels and have to create content and align themselves more closely with the customer than in previous generations.

Marketers, on occasion, may find themselves interacting with customers on a person-to-person basis via online tools such as social media. As more of the purchase journey goes online, marketers will need more awareness in what it takes to drive the purchase forward which, in many sectors, was previously left to salespeople. Ultimately, this requires closer alignment between sales and marketing departments than there generally has been [2].

Notes

1 Dictionary.com (nd) Sell [sel] [online] www.dictionary.com/browse/sell (archived at https://perma.cc/FMF3-8NNB) [accessed 08 March 2018]

2 Sindle, J (2014) Smarketing: the convergence of social, sales and marketing, *Modern Marketing Today*, 16 April [online] modernmarketingtoday.com/smarketing-the-convergence-of-social-sales-and-marketing/ (archived at https://perma.cc/MC72-X9WU) [accessed 29 March 2018]

MYTH
4

I DON'T NEED MARKETING – MY COMPANY IS TOO SMALL AND BUSINESS COMES FROM WORD OF MOUTH

Consider a small business in its very early stages. The founder, or founders, of the company would start the business by deciding what products or services they were going to provide. They would determine the scope of the offering, how and where the product or service would be accessed, the way it would be delivered and the price they were going to charge.

In terms of the 'marketing mix', using the acronym CAVE – Communication, Access, Value and Experience – as established in Myth 2, our business founders have already considered:

Experience – the product or service on offer, the scope of the offering and how it is going to be delivered.

Access – in what format the offering will be provided and where it will be available.

Value – the price they are going to charge and what the customer receives for the money they spend.

These strategic aspects of marketing are essential to the existence of an organization and yet they are often not perceived as marketing at all. It is what led Peter Drucker, one of the most influential thinkers on business management, to write in his book, *The Practice of Management*: 'Because the purpose of business is to create a customer, the business enterprise has two – and only two – basic functions: marketing and innovation. Marketing and innovation produce results; all the rest are costs. Marketing is the distinguishing, unique function of the business' [1].

When company owners declare they 'don't do any marketing' it is incorrect. In the early stages of an enterprise, the business leaders will continually re-evaluate and iterate the offering until they feel it is exactly right. Not only are they carrying out marketing, but it may well be their main focus.

What they mean, of course, is that they don't put any significant resource into the 'Communication' aspect of marketing. But actually, there is likely to have been some investment of time and money into this area. Most organizations will create a logo or company identity. It is probable they will build a website, however simple, and possibly ensure they have a presence on some relevant social media platforms. So, if they don't need marketing, why engage in any of those activities?

We've now debunked the myth of a business not needing, or being too small for marketing. However, in terms of 'Communication' there is a rationale to this claim which, while misguided, can be understood.

In some cases, a business owner will start their company by directly approaching old colleagues, customers from when they worked in a previous role and other contacts. It will often be through these personal communications that an organization will gain its first clients. As we explored in Myth 3, personal selling is a form of communication and, therefore, strictly speaking a subset of marketing. Nevertheless, it is a distinct activity. It might well be that a business grows quite significantly with personal selling as the only meaningful channel of communication.

At this stage in the development of an enterprise, it is likely that all the strategic marketing decisions will be made by the owners of the company. Many people wrongly associate marketing with communications and nothing more, and may not perceive these strategic decisions as marketing. Meanwhile, their customers might be coming from personal selling. Consequently, a business owner may declare that they 'don't need marketing'. While we can recognize this is untrue, we can understand why they are making this claim.

Similarly, when a business owner asserts that their company is 'too small for marketing', what they inadvertently mean is that the marketing activities are not significant enough to warrant a specific employee or separate department dedicated to this one area. As we have determined, the enterprise would have, by necessity, engaged in marketing activities.

The final claim, that the company does not need marketing because all the business comes from 'word of mouth' is interesting. A lot of strategic marketing decisions will have been taken in order to create an offering that is good enough for people to recommend. Marketing will have contributed to any word of mouth referrals that a company receives. In a digital age, though, there are other aspects concerning word of mouth to consider.

Word of mouth has always been extremely important to any business. 'Nielsen reports that the most meaningful form of advertising is recommendations from friends and family: 83 per cent of consumers in 60 countries say they trust these recommendations over any other form of advertising' [2]. This is because social proof, that is, what other people say and do, is one of the biggest influencers on human behaviour [3]. The success of multitudes of enterprises can be attributed to word of mouth.

In an analogue age it was difficult to be strategic about word of mouth. Companies could deliver the best experience possible to customers and hope this led to recommendations. Individuals may have asked satisfied customers whether they would refer them to others, with varying success. Representatives from an enterprise could attend networking events where people were encouraged to become familiar with both attendees and their offerings and refer them to their networks. Of course, all of these options involve marketing. That aside, while any of these alternatives may have produced results, they were certainly not approaches that could be relied upon to deliver repeatable outcomes.

Today, this has changed. We now live in a world where everyone can access their own media channel or channels. Consequently, social sharing plays a major part in the dissemination of information, whereby people's friends and colleagues become their content curators. Moreover, comments, thoughts and ideas that were previously shared face to face, or on the telephone, are now received via social platforms and messaging apps. Essentially, word of mouth has gone online.

This represents a huge opportunity for business. Rather than passively waiting for the next referral, and never quite knowing where it is coming from, companies today can both elicit word of mouth and measure it.

The currency of media is content. Therefore, in owning media channels, if today's organizations want their online presence to be effective, they are compelled to produce content that will have value for their target audience. By testing, measuring and iterating what they produce, companies can create material that people engage with, comment on and share with others. How much engagement and comments a particular piece of content receives, and how many times it is shared, are all metrics that can be easily measured. By producing the right material, organizations can generate word of mouth on an ongoing basis.

While someone sharing a video or article with a friend is not a referral in the literal sense, it is nevertheless a tacit endorsement. For example, if a company produces a video containing insights of how to achieve an outcome more effectively, and a person shares it with a colleague, there is an inference that the company itself is good. Therefore, not only was marketing necessary to obtain word of mouth referrals in an analogue age, in the digital world it can be used to effectively generate and receive more word of mouth than was previously possible.

Consequently, a lack of representation could severely damage a company's ability to win business and compete. An organization requires marketing to provide this online presence. The combination of social sharing as one of the major ways information is disseminated together with purchase journeys going online, means that prospects and customers are no longer merely an audience to be targeted. Today they are also a major channel to market. While prospects and customers could choose to share experiences of their own volition, the idea of a company providing opportunities for its target market to engage, get involved, comment and share, seems compelling. Of course, it is marketing that will enable this to happen.

An increasing majority of purchase journeys have either partially or completely migrated online [4]. Buyers are using search engines, websites, social search, customer reviews, comments and testimonials, personal networks, online videos, online communities, blogs and social platforms in order to make buying decisions. The result is that for a company to receive word-of-mouth recommendations it is increasingly required to have an active online presence – in other words, a marketing activity. All enterprises, however small, undertook some marketing even when business was almost exclusively generated from word-of-mouth referrals. The move to digital means that to ensure it still receives those recommendations, an organization has to engage in more overt marketing activities than in previous times.

Notes

1 Drucker, P F (1955) *The Practice of Management*, Routledge, London
2 Bernazzani, S (2017) Marketing: 20 examples of social proof in action [blog] *Hubspot*, 9 August [online] blog.hubspot.com/marketing/social-proof-examples (archived at https://perma.cc/FXZ5-9NJY) [accessed 29 March 2018]

3 Psychology Notes (2015) What is the Social Proof Theory? The Psychology Notes HQ – Online resources for psychology students, 31 August [online] www.psychologynoteshq.com/social-proof/ (archived at https://perma.cc/HEN2-YSQQ) [accessed 29 March 2018]

4 Forrester Consulting (2016) Why search + social = success for brands. The role of search and social in the customer life cycle [online] www.catalystdigital.com/wp-content/uploads/WhySearchPlusSocialEqualsSuccess-Catalyst.pdf (archived at https://perma.cc/M64S-XAR4) [accessed 09 March 2018]

I DON'T NEED A MARKETING PLAN

Whatever products or services a business offers, there will be a plan to guarantee these can be delivered. From ensuring that the company has the necessary equipment, to providing the appropriate number of staff, or making certain it is adhering to the compulsory legal requirements and regulations, an enterprise will make preparations to meet its customers' demands.

Yet when it comes to attracting and winning clients, too many companies undertake this in an ad hoc and haphazard way. This can result in all sorts of challenges. Enterprises will sometimes find they simply don't have enough customers to be commercially viable. A company may be forced to take work that isn't entirely appropriate or reduce prices just to enable the business to survive.

Many organizations experience peaks and troughs, whereby they are so busy that they don't undertake any proactive marketing communications. The result is that when the work calms down, they simply don't have enough business. They then accelerate the marketing and sales activities, which brings in opportunities and the whole cycle starts again.

Quite simply, without customers there is no enterprise. The very survival of a business, and its growth, depends on a company's ability to acquire and retain an ever-increasing number of people who will buy its products and services. Just as operationally an organization won't leave the delivery of its products and services to chance, it makes no sense to risk the viability of the company itself by failing to plan for the acquisition of customers.

In order to keep customers, and constantly attract new ones, an organization will need to continually assess factors such as the changing market, the opportunities that it provides and the resource it has to exploit this ever-changeable situation. It will need to choose the measures by which it will determine how successful it is in fulfilling its set objectives and identify the mechanisms to enable it to reach its defined goals.

In short, a business requires a marketing strategy and a plan to execute it, without which it is unlikely to achieve much success. There are so many considerations that need to be taken into account to ensure a company is able to 'obtain and retain' customers, that it seems absurd for any organization to try to achieve this without a defined strategy and plan.

When putting a marketing strategy together there are external factors, which must be evaluated. This can be undertaken using the mnemonic STEEPLE [1], a variation on PEST first developed by Harvard Professor Francis Aguilar in 1967 [2]. The components of STEEPLE should be considered in helping to ascertain who should be targeted, the value in the offering and its sustainability, as well as factors that could provide additional threats or opportunities. The mnemonic consists of:

Social – cultural changes such as population, demographics, health, the workplace, lifestyles and fashion.

Technological – technological changes including new technologies, those becoming obsolete and the impact of these developments.

Economic – growth, inflation, exchange rates, interest rates, general confidence and unemployment.

Environmental – weather, climate change and regulation.

Political – tax, employment, trade restrictions and tariffs as well as stability and how all aspects of government policy may affect business.

Legal – health and safety, discrimination, employment, consumer, competition and antitrust laws which affect the business environment.

Ethical – changing social values and their impact.

Having considered these external elements, it is useful for a business to look internally and consider the strengths and weaknesses of the organization. Factors to be considered are:

- the management team and its ability;
- the level of employees and their capability;
- internal processes, information systems and quality standards;
- suppliers – the reliance on them, and how they affect the company's ability to deliver internally and externally;
- internal communications and productivity;
- its financial position.

With a clear understanding of these internal and external factors a business can then deliberate the actual marketing issues that must be evaluated as part of the plan. We will explore these using the acronym CAVE, outlined in Myth 2.

Perhaps the best place to start is with E – experience. This encompasses the product or service in its totality. First, there is the product or service itself. What are the challenges that prospects have that this offering is designed to solve? How does it meet current customers' requirements? What are the market trends and external factors that may render the current products or services obsolete, and provide opportunities to innovate and introduce new aspects to the offering?

While considering the offering, there are other aspects that must be contemplated. Competitors should be taken into account together with their relative strengths and weaknesses. Where does the business have competitive advantage? Where could it create competitive advantage?

While addressing 'experience' a business must think about differentiation. In the commoditized world in which we live, businesses don't usually differentiate by 'what' they do. Instead, they often differentiate by 'who' they do it for. Therefore, this consideration creates the requirement for a business to think about 'who' it is targeting and further market segmentation.

Differentiation often comes by creating an amazing 'how' for the specific target market, even if 'what' a company does is similar to others. For example, an HR consultancy specializing in working with manufacturing businesses still performs all the expected services any HR consultancy would deliver. Therefore, it is not different in 'what' it does. However, by concentrating on working with manufacturers, it may be able to produce specialist guidelines, utilize specific and relevant case studies and provide a deeper understanding of market trends that are particular to running production lines and employing a significant number of blue-collar workers. In other words, 'how' it delivers its service is adapted to the distinct marketplace it serves.

An organization must also think about its market positioning and how it wants to be perceived in the mind of the customer. For example, our HR consultancy might use the line, 'the number one choice of UK manufacturers', giving it a clear position in the market. This, of course, leads into the wider consideration of the company's brand and what it represents.

All of these factors are too strategic to try to make sense of in a haphazard way. Many companies' marcom activities are ineffective because they haven't segmented their prospects adequately and they fail to establish a strong market position or distinctive offer. Without a real understanding of customer challenges and how those influence the messaging an organization uses, and the value it provides, there is a good chance that communications won't resonate with prospects and have the impact necessary to attract the desired number of customers. In short, a marketing plan forces a business to think through the necessary strategic issues which will provide it with a much greater chance of success.

Having developed the 'experience', a company will need to consider A – access. This is the different means by which a prospect and customer will interact with, purchase or receive the product or service. Although it is a distinct factor in its own right, the way a person accesses a product or service will contribute to the experience. For example, is it only available online? Are there different online or offline aspects? Does a customer have to travel to a particular place or does it come to them?

These considerations will also affect the next element which is V – value. This consists of the price charged, the time and effort a purchase takes, the expenditure necessary to implement the solution and any costs of ownership and maintenance, in relation to what the customer receives. The context in which a purchase occurs must also be taken into account. For example, a person is likely to be prepared to pay more for a cold soft drink when lying on the beach, than when doing the weekly shop in a supermarket.

Contemplating value will require a company to address its pricing strategy. It will have to consider profitability, comparisons in the market and its positioning. For example, if a product is positioned as best in class it is unlikely to be the cheapest, as customers expect to pay more for quality. If positioning and pricing don't work together it can lead to an incongruence which may result in the offering being distrusted and failing. Any discounts and offers will also have to be thought through as part of the value element of the marketing strategy.

C – communication – is the final part of the marketing mix to be addressed. An organization must really understand buyer motivations in order to craft messages that will allure prospects into making a purchase. Having established its core messages, a company will have to decide which channels to utilize in order to reach its target market. From TV to social media, direct mail to strategic partnerships, an organization has a plethora of options.

Too many companies without a marketing plan use channels such as social media, direct mail and their own website in a purely tactical way. They flitter from one campaign, or promotion, to another while trying to achieve a return on investment for the time and money spent. By having a proper plan in place, companies can obtain more from their efforts by ensuring that activities in the various channels are joined up and complement each other. This will render each one more effective.

As well as creating market awareness, a company will have to determine how it converts attention into customers. It could be by obtaining distribution into the right retail outlets, creating an e-commerce platform or through personal selling. Strategies for customer retention will also need to be considered, with anything from employing individuals to personally manage accounts, to loyalty programmes and newsletters etc, being utilized.

A business may not have all the information it requires to reach conclusions on any of the considerations above. Therefore, it may choose to undertake market research in any number of specific areas to help inform any conclusions that are reached.

It should be apparent from the complexities involved in putting together an effective marketing strategy, and being able to implement it, that an organization requires the creation of a plan. There are other aspects of a marketing plan that require it to be formalized.

Resources must be allocated in order to fulfil the plan. For example, budgets will be required to deliver the communications. There may be a need for training or a necessity to recruit new employees. It may also be essential to expand or change the capability in production or service delivery.

In order to motivate staff, assign roles and responsibilities and manage performance, the plan and its goals will need to be communicated to everyone in the organization. Whether this is a very small team or a company employing thousands, it will be difficult to articulate the plan without it being in some tangible form.

Finally, measures, or key performance indicators (KPIs), will have to be put in place in order to be able to evaluate and monitor results. When putting these measures together it is worth remembering the mnemonic SMART, created by George Doran in 1981 [3]. It ensures measures are:

S – specific – is a precise aspect that is monitored with good reason.

M – measurable – there must be indicators in order to monitor progress.

A – assignable – there is a person or persons responsible for results.

R – realistic – that the objective is possible.

T – time bound – has to be delivered within a particular period.

A marketing plan should not be static. It should be reviewed regularly. By having appropriate measures in place, progress can be monitored and tweaks and changes can be made in order to improve results. In producing a comprehensive marketing plan, a company will be able to continually iterate, based on the measures it has in place, and in this way maximize the positive effects of any marketing efforts.

Notes

1 Sloman, J and Jones, E (2011) *Economics and the Business Environment,* Financial Times/Prentice Hall as an imprint of Pearson, London
2 Frue, K (2017) Who invented PEST analysis and why it matters, *Pestle Analysis*, 8 May [online] https://pestleanalysis.com/who-invented-pest-analysis/ (archived at https://perma.cc/3ZS7-53UD) [accessed 11 March 2018]
3 Haughey, D (2014) A brief history of smart goals, *Project Smart*, 13 December [online] www.projectsmart.co.uk/brief-history-of-smart-goals.php (archived at https://perma.cc/PQZ4-39WQ) [accessed 11 March 2018]

MYTH
6

MARKETING IS SOLELY THE RESPONSIBILITY OF THE MARKETING DEPARTMENT

Peter Drucker, one of the most influential figures on business theory, wrote in his book *The Practice of Management*: 'Because the purpose of business is to create a customer, the business enterprise has two – and only two – basic functions: marketing and innovation. Marketing and innovation produce results; all the rest are costs. Marketing is the distinguishing, unique function of the business' [1].

If marketing goes to the very core of a business, how can the responsibility for it resolve in one part of the organization? Looking at the traditional marketing mix, it seems ludicrous that all these areas would be left to one department. If they were, the chief marketing officer would be de facto running the entire organization, which is not the case.

While determining the product or service offering and continually ensuring that it is compelling for customers is a marketing discipline, it is absurd to think that these decisions would be taken solely by the marketing department. Innovations and ideas for iterating offerings, and creating new ones, will often be the responsibility of a separate team. For instance, many organizations today have created innovation hubs [2]. Deciding on the scope of a business offering goes right to the heart of what a company does. There are likely to be a number of strategic leaders in an organization who will have a valid view and want a say in the decisions that are made.

The requirement to ensure that there is capability to implement an idea will mean that the person in charge of customer service, or operations, will need to be involved. New offerings have to be funded, which then introduces the chief financial officer into the equation. While customer experience is technically a marketing discipline, there will be many people and departments participating. From sales to finance, account management to customer service teams, receptionists to delivery drivers, there will be numerous touchpoints and interactions which will affect the customer and their view of the offering.

How a customer interacts with, and purchases, a product or service is another part of the marketing mix which will not solely be decided by a marketing department. It is a decision that goes to the heart of business strategy and other senior decision makers within an enterprise will want to provide their view. There are lots of operational considerations that will impinge on other departments. For example, any online delivery and e-commerce offering will make it likely that the views of the head of IT will need to be considered. In fact, the growing importance of technology in marketing with customer relationship management systems, marketing automation, artificial intelligence and augmented and virtual reality, to name but a few areas, means that often the marketing department must work closely with the technological team in a business.

The value a buyer receives, which encompasses balancing the offer to the customer with all the costs of purchasing, implementing, owning and maintaining any solution, is also a marketing discipline. Yet it is unimaginable that in most companies marketing would solely be responsible for pricing strategy without, for example, the chief financial officer having a view.

The three parts of the marketing mix that we have sighted so far are areas in which the marketing department should be involved. The fact that they go to the very heart of the strategy of the business is exactly Peter Drucker's point; it is preposterous to think that sole responsibility for these decisions would reside in one department.

The part of the marketing mix most commonly (and broadly) termed marketing communications is the area where marketers tend to have the most autonomy. But even within this remit, there are many aspects which are simply too important to leave solely to the marketing department.

While the marketing team tend to be the brand guardians in an organization, there are many aspects of the brand that are so strategic the senior decision makers have to be involved. Defining the company purpose, value proposition, emotional proposition and market positioning all directly affect the way an organization communicates with its audience. However, in order to be authentic, these values have to come from the founders or leaders of the business [3]. They cannot simply be determined by marketing personnel, working in a silo, and then imposed on the rest of the enterprise.

Determining what a company stands for and its market positioning starts to impinge on considerations such as how an organization differentiates itself, which, in turn, introduces matters such as targeting and market segmentation. Of course, the marketing department should participate in these deliberations. In fact, the market research and analysis, which is often used to inform these decisions, is normally embarked upon, or commissioned, by the marketing team.

Undertaking research into the market, analysing the competition, obtaining customer feedback from interviews, polls and surveys and listening to conversations on social channels are all areas for which marketing is usually responsible. However, customer insights will also reside elsewhere in an organization. For example, a sales team, or customer service department, will also have knowledge which will need to be shared. Data which will provide customer insight will also exist throughout an organization. A customer service team will have data concerning customer complaints and frequently asked questions. The technical department looking after the e-commerce platform will have data regarding orders and frequency of purchases etc. Of course, all this information is vital in making the right marketing decisions.

While research activities and data analysis will significantly contribute to the conclusions a business reaches regarding differentiation and the targeting of customers, these choices go to the heart of business strategy. A marketing department is unlikely to be left to resolve these issues alone.

The tactical delivery of communications, and the channels used, are normally the areas people believe are the sole remit of marketing. However, this is too simplistic a view. It is true that in the past, promotions and campaigns were often left to marketing departments to execute. Advertising and supporting materials such as brochures and leaflets were also the responsibility of the marketing team, as well as management of the relationships with agencies, print vendors, PR companies, copywriters and designers.

But the ascent of digital means that marketing departments are now running media channels. Like all media, websites and social platforms require constant content. While the marketing department may be responsible for managing these channels, content ideas and contributions often need to come from other areas in a business. For example, it may be senior management personnel who are required to appear on company videos, vlogs and other materials that an enterprise produces.

Social channels blur these lines further. As brand guardians, marketing departments often want to take control of social platforms, creating the material that is posted on them as well as replying to comments. However, customer service teams may well utilize social media to provide quicker and more responsive assistance to consumers. Salespeople will also be using social media. With an ever-increasing amount of the purchase journey going online, it makes sense for salespeople to be interacting with prospects and customers via social platforms.

In many ways, salespeople have always blurred the lines of how much of the communications a marketing department controls. Technically, personal selling is a marketing channel. It is a particular medium for reaching prospects. In many business-to-business organizations it is accepted that buyers are unlikely to purchase expensive products or services without meeting someone from the enterprise. Personal selling has frequently been the key channel in turning opportunities into business. Consequently, sales departments are often a separate entity, working autonomously from the marketing team with their own personnel and budgets. Therefore, a major aspect of the communications of a company has had little to do with marketing.

In fact, it is the importance of 'personal selling' in many business-to-business enterprises that has often left the marketing department being seen as little more than a support function for the sales team [4]. Sometimes this shows itself with marketing being charged with little more than producing supporting materials for salespeople. In other organizations marketing is made responsible for lead generation, with the sales team then being made accountable for closing those opportunities.

Perhaps the farcicality of the marketing department being the only ones responsible for marketing is shown in the outcomes which marketing should achieve. Ultimately, marketing is responsible for obtaining and retaining customers. While a marketing department should be contributing to this outcome, a sales team may also be responsible for achieving this result. When it comes to customer retention, almost every department of a business, in one way or another, will influence the experience a customer has and whether they will want to continue using a particular organization in the future.

If so many aspects of marketing are disseminated throughout an enterprise, then one could reasonably ask, why have a marketing department at all? The answer to this question, however, is to make sure that there is an individual, or team, perennially thinking about marketing issues. If no one person or department is responsible for marketing, the danger is that it is not focused on enough. Having a dedicated resource to this area of business is vital. While this person or department will not realistically be able to manage all facets of marketing, it is important that there is a function within an enterprise that takes some responsibility for this discipline.

Perhaps the overarching value of a marketing department in today's business environment, where consumers are so empowered and have so much access to choice, is that there is a team looking at all aspects of the enterprise from the customer's point of view. While marketing is necessarily disseminated throughout an organization, the dedicated marketing resource should perhaps think of itself as the 'customers' department' and the head of marketing as the chief customer officer. In this way, an enterprise is less likely to lose focus on what it must ultimately achieve to succeed commercially: winning customers and keeping them.

Notes

1 Drucker, P F (1955) *The Practice of Management*, Routledge, London
2 CB Insights (2017) From AT&T to Xerox: 65 corporate innovation labs, CB Insights Research Briefs. 20 May [online] www.cbinsights.com/research/corporate-innovation-labs/ (archived at https://perma.cc/Z7UG-3Q44) [accessed 29 March 2018]
3 Lencioni, P M (2002) Make your values mean something, *Harvard Business Review*, July [online] hbr.org/2002/07/make-your-values-mean-something (archived at https://perma.cc/AJ6G-M5G5) [accessed 11 March 2018]
4 Schwartz, J (2015) Research highlight: the rise of marketing as a strategic function, *ITSMA*, 21 May [online] www.itsma.com/research-highlight-marketing-as-a-strategic-function/ (archived at https://perma.cc/3K4M-G9FW) [accessed 12 March 2018]

ULTIMATELY, PEOPLE BUY ON PRICE

Go into any supermarket car park and you'll see an array of different models on display. Yet if people solely bought on price, logic would suggest that there would only be one type of vehicle on show: the cheapest. Similarly, when booking a long-haul flight, on any conventional airline, a passenger will be offered a range of different classes of cabin. Typically, the scope will include first, business, premium and economy. If price, though, were the ultimate criteria of purchase there would only be one class of ticket: the cheapest.

Despite the tangible evidence that this isn't the case, one frequently meets individuals who seemed to be resigned to the fact that ultimately people only buy their products or services on price. They think that if they want to acquire customers, and sell their goods and services, price is the most significant factor. The reality is that price becomes most important when all the other aspects of a purchase are perceived to be equal. When everything else is the same, price becomes a clear area of difference. It is often a lack of differentiation that leads to a company being squeezed on price.

Of course, price is an important criterion of purchase. Quite simply, there is a question of financial means. There will be an amount of money above which an individual or business will not be able to spend. This may be because of budget allocation, or a simple question of affordability.

As well as the price of purchase, total expenditure will be taken into account when deliberating the cost of an acquisition. For instance, implementing the solution itself may necessitate spend, as a previous product might have to be uninstalled or taken away. There could be a need to train staff. Ownership may also require outlay such as storage or maintenance costs. Any necessary ongoing purchases would also be considered, for example, petrol for a car, cartridges for a printer or a monthly contract for a cell phone.

Despite the price and cost of ownership being an important factor in any buying decision, there are other aspects that are also significant. Any enterprise that understands these other elements, and delivers on them as part of its proposition to a customer, will become less exposed to price pressure.

One consideration that is crucial is the minimizing of risk. No one wants an insurance policy that doesn't pay out, a car that keeps breaking down or a software platform that is unfit for use. Therefore, reputation can play a considerable part in any purchasing decision. People will pay more for a product or service that is widely perceived as trustworthy and reliable. Good peer reviews, testimonials and any other social proof that demonstrates the credentials of an offering, can have a significant influence on a buying decision [1].

This is one of the deliverables that a recognized brand can provide. A brand that is associated with maintaining a good standard of product or service elicits trust and minimizes some of the risk of purchase. Familiarity also provides comfort and reassurance, which is a reason people are often willing to pay more for a brand they recognize [2].

Emotion will also play a large part in any buying decision. As Peter Noel Murray points out: 'Emotion is a necessary ingredient to almost all decisions. When we are confronted with a decision, emotions from previous, related experiences affix values to the options we are considering. These emotions create preferences, which lead to our decision' [3]. This, of course, includes risk (the fear of it not working out), as well as the aspirations, wants or dreams of an individual or organization.

Purchases are often made in order to evoke feelings, whether it is an individual spending a day at a spa to feel pampered and cared for, buying an expensive watch or car to feel important, stylish and successful, or an organization providing staff with the latest cell phones to reinforce the sense internally of it being a great company to work for and a market leader.

An offering that delivers the right feelings to a prospect may also find them less price sensitive. This is, again, where investing in a brand makes commercial sense. People will be willing to pay more for a brand that will usually be able to deliver the emotion better than an unrecognized competitor. For example, could an unknown pair of trainers deliver the same feelings of being a winner as Nike does?

Convenience is another factor that can have a considerable influence on a purchasing decision [4]. Anything which reduces the time and effort that is needed, is capable of having a huge impact. From a software product that requires very little in the way of learning in order to use it, to a takeaway meal that is delivered rather than needing to be collected, buyers are often willing to pay more to save on any of their own endeavours.

All of this amounts to people buying on 'value', that is the worth that something provides for them against the costs incurred, rather than on price alone. As Warren Buffet said, 'Price is what you pay, value is what you get' [5]. Of course, different people are likely to have a contrasting perception of value, which is why segmenting and targeting the market is so important.

For example, a family with a finite budget for a holiday may not value business class travel. The relatively short time spent on the plane, compared with the rest of the vacation, may mean that they are willing to go economy class to their destination and have more money to spend on the hotel and other activities. In contrast, the main consideration for an individual travelling long haul, for a relatively short business trip, could be that they arrive as prepared as possible for their meetings. Being able to sleep and eat well on the plane, as well as having space to work comfortably, might result in a business class ticket providing extremely good value for them.

Conveying the appropriate value to the right purchaser is vital to commercial success. Not all customers will consider all the attributes of an offering as equally important. While being able to sleep on the flight might be vital to the individual travelling on business, it may not even be a consideration for a family on holiday intent on watching as many movies as possible. Understanding buyer motivations is key to all aspects of a company's marketing being successful.

This example also highlights another dynamic which changes the perception of value. If the expenditure accounts for a large percentage of the budget available, then the compromises needed to make the purchase will be more significant. Therefore, the value has to be greater than when a purchase represents a smaller amount of resource. So, our family could afford to fly business class, although it would have taken a significant amount of their holiday budget. This would have resulted in them having to cut back on meals and activities at their destination. This sacrifice meant that, in value terms, it wasn't deemed worthwhile. If this family had a much larger holiday budget and the business class tickets, in relative terms, were a much smaller percentage of that budget, requiring much less forfeiting of other activities at their destination, their perception of value may have changed.

Where price is fixed, value is relative, and the impression of whether an offering provides value or not can be altered by other factors. A good example of this is the context in which a purchase takes place. An ice cream seller, wheeling a small freezer full of ice creams, may charge three times the standard price of a given product. If this salesperson wheels the freezer down a beach in the summertime many people may gladly buy an ice cream. The relative value of an ice cream goes up when one is on a beach in the hot weather and a good walk away from any other options. The seller may not find buyers as receptive walking along the promenade, by the beach, on a much cooler day. The change in temperature and circumstances will alter the perception of value even though the price stays the same.

In this scenario, as the context of the purchase changed, the perception of what was a 'fair' or 'reasonable' price altered. People will often have an idea of what they think they should pay. Regardless of whether this is an educated estimate or a complete guess, this frame of reference will change the impression of whether a prospect is getting value or not. Reference points can come from online research, chats with friends or context. For example, if someone is purchasing a pair of headphones to use with their cell phone which cost $200, a pair of headphones also costing $200 may seem excessive. It is not that the headphones are not worth $200 in their own right but, because they are a mere accessory to the main item, in relative terms, the price seems high.

Alternatively, when a buyer is making a purchase of a luxury or exclusive item, a higher price is part of the value proposition. These items are bought in order to feel indulgent and bring status and distinction to the purchaser. It is because of the relatively high price that the item delivers this value. Of course, there is a question of affordability and a business must know its target market, but people are likely to be less price sensitive in this scenario.

The number of suppliers in a market, and the variety of options a buyer feels they have, will also affect their perception of value. The more alternatives there are, the less value a prospect is likely to see in any particular one. This is especially true when the offerings are very similar. As mentioned at the beginning of the myth, the only distinguishing factor left will then be the prices charged.

Conversely, the fewer choices a buyer has, and the more difficult it becomes to compare the different options, the more value a prospect is likely to see in a proposition. A company that truly differentiates, and creates clear blue water between itself and competitors, is likely to face less price pressure as it will be seen to provide more value. This can be achieved by creating a unique offering, or through the market segmentation and targeting of a specific audience. It may not be what a company does that makes it different, but rather who it does it for that creates value for the customer and consequently prevents price being the most important criteria of purchase.

Notes

1 Campbell, C (2016) Online reviews are the new social proof, *Entrepreneur*, 27 September [online] www.entrepreneur.com/article/281600 (archived at https://perma.cc/GS6G-NRML) [accessed 12 March 2018]

2 Course Hero (nd) A brand helps reduce a buyer's perceived risk of purchase [online] https://www.coursehero.com/file/149632/Marketing-Exam-2-Notes/ (archived at https://perma.cc/5KTW-KTGM) [accessed 29 March 2018]

3 Murray, P N (2013) How emotions influence what we buy: the emotional core of consumer decision-making. *Psychology Today*, 26 February [online] www.psychologytoday.com/blog/inside-the-consumer-mind/201302/how-emotions-influence-what-we-buy (archived at https://perma.cc/7GYS-TCHS) [accessed 14 March 2018]

4 Kelley, E J (1958) The importance of convenience in consumer purchasing, convenience forms and marketing theory, *Journal of Marketing, American Marketing Association*, July [online] www.jstor.org/stable/1248014?seq=1#page_scan_tab_contents (archived at https://perma.cc/U87A-547R) [accessed 14 March 2018]

5 Wiley (nd) The Warren Buffet Way – Warren buffet quotes [online] www.wiley.com/WileyCDA/Section/id-817935.html (archived at https://perma.cc/3M33-C3N2) [accessed 14 March 2018]

MYTH
8

PRICING IS A MATTER OF CHARGING THE HIGHEST AMOUNT POSSIBLE

One of the considerations an organization will have to deliberate is its revenue model. For example, an enterprise can have a straight-forward system of charging for the goods and services that it sells, and there are a variety of ways of accomplishing this. The amount can be taken as a simple, one-off transaction or alternatively, there is a whole array of other payment options like renting or leasing, charging commissions or subscription services.

It's important to think carefully about payment options. Research conducted by John T Gourville, a professor at Harvard Business School, and Dilip Soman, a professor at Hong Kong University of Science and Technology, demonstrated that how a company charges can affect consumption and retention. For example, it is more likely that an individual will consistently use a gym if they are charged $100 per month rather than $1,200 at the beginning of the year. Although the person charged the full amount up front is likely to use it more at the beginning, as the time of the payment gets further away it is probable that their usage will reduce [1].

In general, we tend to consume closer to the time that we pay [1]. As a result, the person making regular payments is prone to use the gym consistently and is more likely to renew their membership. Conversely, if a company wants people to consume less, they are better off charging one large amount. For example, if, on arrival at a busy theme park, people are charged $250 for five separate $50 one-day passes, it is expected that people will go every day. However, if it charges $250 for a five-day pass there is more chance that individuals will be willing to skip a day to do something else [1].

A company may decide not to charge directly at all. Media businesses often use an advertising model whereby a significant amount of its revenue, or in some cases all of its income, is generated by selling advertising to companies targeting the audience it has amassed. Newspapers, magazines, radio and TV networks are typical examples, as are web companies such as Google, Facebook and Twitter [2].

A lot of web companies utilize a 'freemium' model, whereby the basic product or service, such as software, games or content, can be used free of charge. Users then pay to access advanced features, additional functionality or related offerings [3].

Equally important will be the objectives a company wants to achieve in setting its price. 'Price skimming' is used when a company has a competitive advantage in the market due to innovation [4]. New products, when they are released, are normally aimed at early adopters. This has been the case with innovations in the past such as digital watches, DVD players and smart phones. By keeping the price high, companies require fewer sales to break even. 'Price skimming' can be used to recover some of the investment costs in the development of a product. As new entrants inevitably come into the market, and the product becomes more widespread, this pricing policy is not usually sustainable and eventually has to be changed.

'Loss leaders', whereby a product is sold at a low price, is a strategy often used by retailers, etailers and supermarkets to try to increase market share [5]. This can often be at cost, or even below cost, and this attracts customers into a store or onto a website. The aim is that this traffic will lead to a greater number of profitable sales of other goods.

Similarly, 'penetration pricing' is another approach to capture market share [6]. The price of goods or services is set deliberately low to attract customers. Once a certain market share is achieved, a company may well then raise prices. This technique is often used by new entrants into a market. Utilities companies and broadband providers are examples of businesses that have utilized penetration pricing in order to encourage people to switch suppliers.

There are a number of revenue management strategies used by companies in order to maximize profit which do not necessarily mean charging one single arbitrary price. 'Price discrimination' involves setting a different price, for the same offering, in distinctive segments of the market [7], for example, charging separate prices for adults and children.

'Price differentiation' means charging a different price for the same offering, when the circumstances change. For instance, one may receive an early bird discount for making a commitment and booking a long time in advance. Another example is that it may be more expensive to go and see a movie on a Saturday night as opposed to a Tuesday afternoon.

While 'price discrimination' makes a distinction between customers and 'price differentiation' distinguishes circumstances, 'dynamic pricing' allows companies to sell the same offering, in the same circumstances, to the same customer at different prices based on demand [8]. With 'price discrimination' and 'price differentiation' prices are static and set in advance. However, 'dynamic pricing' is used to manage demand and maximize profits by making tactical adjustments to the price throughout the sales cycle.

Both 'differential pricing' and 'dynamic pricing' were first used in aviation. The idea of dynamic pricing is often credited to Robert Crandall, a former president and chairman of American Airlines [9]. Today, carriers use advanced software to forecast demand and optimize price and inventory [10]. They can then offer lower prices on flights that are unlikely to sell out in order to increase demand, and charge much higher prices to take advantage when demand is high. 'Yield management' involves increasing prices at peak times to further improve earnings [11].

When companies have a variety of offerings, ensuring the 'product line pricing' is right so customers see the value in the various options is important. For instance, a car wash will have escalating charges for more thorough packages. So, a basic exterior wash, an exterior wash and interior vacuum clean, and finally an exterior wash, interior clean together with a protective hand-polished wax, will be priced at increasingly higher amounts. There are many techniques companies utilize when it comes to product pricing.

A method widely used by airlines and hotels is 'optional product pricing' [12]. This is where the cost of the basic product, for example an airline ticket, is offered at a relatively low price, and optional extras then increase the cost. Typical instances with airlines would be preferential seating, extra baggage, food and beverages etc.

A similar idea is 'captive product pricing' [13]. Again, the initial core product is priced relatively low with higher prices then charged for the 'captive product'. There are many examples of this; for instance, companies will sell printers at a low price but charge more for the cartridges [14].

'Product bundle pricing', where enterprises group products together, so they are cheaper than if bought individually, is another technique used to increase customer spend [15]. There are various examples such as value meals at restaurants, alternative options when buying a new car and viewing packages from entertainment companies such as Netflix.

Some of these techniques start to veer into the area of 'psychological pricing', which uses knowledge of human psychology in order to make offers and prices look as attractive as possible to buyers [16]. For example, 'product bundle pricing' often leads to an increase in customer spend because it is easier for an individual to justify a single upgrade rather than having to consider the purchase of a number of individual items [17].

Special offers often encourage people to spend more as they feel they are getting a deal. Giving away items for 'free' frequently works well because people generally overvalue the benefits of 'free' [18]. There are a large number of examples of 'free offers' such as getting a free biscuit with your coffee, free delivery when you spend over $20, and of course the famous BOGOF – 'buy one get one free'.

'Psychological pricing' can make a big difference when setting 'product line prices' [19]. For example, 'anchoring' is the word used to describe the human inclination to rely on the first piece of information, 'the anchor', when making decisions [20]. Therefore, a $75 meal suddenly seems good value if the first offering is $125. Similarly, a $300 dress is attractive if the first dress looked at was $700.

Context also matters when setting product line prices. At the beginning of his book, *Predictably Irrational*, author Dan Ariely describes three subscription offers for *The Economist* magazine:

1 Web only – $59.

2 Print only – $125.

3 Print and web – $125 [21].

Obviously, the middle offer is redundant. If you want the print subscription you might as well choose print and web for the same price. When Dan Ariely gave these options to 100 students at MIT's Sloan School of Management, 84 chose the third option. However, when he took the second option away, 68 students chose the web-only option and only 32 chose the print and web. Everything is relative and the second 'redundant offer' made the third option seem better value and was there solely to increase customer spend.

Perhaps the most well-known psychological pricing technique is 'charm pricing'. This is when an item is priced at $7.99 instead of $8.00. This works for two reasons. First, there is what is known as the left digit effect. We scan numbers from left to right and seven is a lower number than eight. Psychologically, we instantly perceive

$7.99 as significantly less than $8.00. Of course, when we rationalize it we realize the difference is meaningless, but the impact of the first perception carries weight [22].

Second, the number nine influences us as we have become culturally conditioned to associate the number nine with bargains and deals. This is deeply ingrained. In an experiment conducted by Duncan Simester of MIT and Eric Anderson of the University of Chicago, a mail-order company printed various versions of its catalogues. It charged three different amounts for the same item of women's clothing $44, $39 and $34. Surprisingly, the item charged at $39 not only outsold the $44 price tag but also the $34 one as well [23]. In his book, *Priceless*, author William Poundstone found that charm pricing increased sales on average by 24 per cent against rounded price points [24].

'Premium or prestige pricing' works in exactly the opposite way [25]. This is the strategy of keeping prices high in order to make the offering feel expensive and distinctive. This strategy is often used with luxury items such as perfumes, high-end fashion and certain brands of cars and watches. Emotionally, these items are often purchased in order for people to feel indulgent, successful, important or distinguished. According to a study for the *Journal of Consumer Research* by Monica Wadhwa and Kuangjie Zhang, these purchases, which are so feelings based, are more attractive with round numbers as they rely on less cognition to process and just 'feel right' [26].

This introduces the idea of market positioning and pricing. If the market positioning of an offering is that it is a luxury item, it requires a high price in order to fulfil that promise. Alternatively, if a company's market position is to always provide great value to customers, the price charged has to be perceived as a good deal, or the whole proposition to the customer breaks down.

When one considers price, in terms of market positioning, competitor charges should also be evaluated. For example, if the market position of an enterprise is to have the most luxurious offering, it may well need to be the most expensive to reinforce this perception. Similarly, when selling knowledge and expertise, pricing too low against the competition could leave customers feeling that the organization is inferior to other providers rather than seeing it as a good deal. The effect on perception must be deliberated when setting price. Pricing strategy, therefore, isn't merely about charging the highest amount that customers are willing to pay. There are so many other aspects that must be considered to ensure the right price is set.

Notes

1 Gourville, J T, Soman, D (2002) Pricing and the psychology of consumption, *Harvard Business Review*, October [online] hbr. org/2002/09/pricing-and-the-psychology-of-consumption (archived at https://perma.cc/UP57-DB8J) [accessed 03 April 2018]

2 Satell, G (2016) As the media industry evolves, the business model becomes the message, *Forbes*, 31 January [online] www.forbes. com/sites/gregsatell/2016/01/31/as-the-media-industry-evolves-the-business-model-becomes-the-message/#6b05bbab3ccd (archived at https://perma.cc/69TV-UFTA) [accessed 01 May 2018]

3 Investopedia (nd) Definition of 'Fremium' [online] www. investopedia.com/terms/f/freemium.asp (archived at https://perma.cc/ DE8N-LMNR) [accessed 03 April 2018]

4 Investopedia (nd) What is 'price skimming', [online] www. investopedia.com/terms/p/priceskimming.asp (archived at https:// perma.cc/VJC5-DBW8) [accessed 03 April 2018]

5 Inc. encyclopedia (nd) Loss leader pricing [online] www.inc.com/ encyclopedia/loss-leader-pricing.html (archived at https://perma.cc/ QF67-VBLN) [accessed 03 April 2018]

6 Business Directory (nd) Market penetration pricing – definition [online] www.businessdictionary.com/definition/market-penetration-pricing.html (archived at https://perma.cc/YP64-QNN6) [accessed 03 April 2018]

7 Tutor2u (nd) Monopoly-price discrimination [online] www.tutor2u. net/economics/reference/monopoly-price-discrimination (archived at https://perma.cc/Q87W-Z57Y) [accessed 01 May 2018]

8 Ecommerce Wiki (nd) What is dynamic pricing? [online] www.ecommercewiki.org/Dynamic_Pricing/Dynamic_Pricing_Basic/ What_is_Dynamic_Pricing (archived at https://perma.cc/93WC-F7V2) [accessed 01 May 2018]

9 McAfee, R P and te Velde, V California Institute of Technology, Dynamic Pricing in the Airline Industry [online] mcafee.cc/Papers/ PDF/DynamicPriceDiscrimination.pdf (archived at https://perma.cc/ Z4Z5-XDFE) [accessed 03 April 2018]

10 Belobaba, P P, Brunger, W G and Wittman, M D (2017) Advances in airline pricing, revenue management, and distribution: implications for the airline industry [online] https://www.atpco.net/sites/atpco-public/files/2019-03/pods-summary-paper.pdf (archived at https://perma.cc/B82J-J7HC) [accessed 03 April 2018]

11 Investorwords (nd) Yield management, definition [online] www.investorwords.com/8736/yield_management.html (archived at https://perma.cc/A3LX-U9MQ) [accessed 01 May 2018]

12 Price Intelligently (nd) Optional product pricing [online] www.priceintelligently.com/optional-product-pricing (archived at https://perma.cc/PW4F-EJVW) [accessed 05 April 2018]

13 Business Directory (nd) Captive product, definition [online] www.businessdictionary.com/definition/captive-product.html (archived at https://perma.cc/6U4K-KQLG) [accessed 03 April 2018]

14 Anderson, C (nd) What is captive product pricing? *Chron.com* [online] smallbusiness.chron.com/captive-product-pricing-18657.html (archived at https://perma.cc/FC5W-MEBY) [accessed 03 April 2018]

15 Business Dictionary (nd) Product bundle pricing, definition [online] www.businessdictionary.com/definition/product-bundle-pricing.html (archived at https://perma.cc/4AME-M6TW) [accessed 03 April 2018]

16 Boachie, P (2016) 5 strategies of 'psychological pricing', *Entrepreneur*, 21 July [online] www.entrepreneur.com/article/279464 (archived at https://perma.cc/N9QD-J8MG) [accessed 04 April 2018]

17 Tjan, A K (2010) The pros and cons of bundled pricing, *Harvard Business Review*, 26 February [online] hbr.org/2010/02/

the-pros-and-cons-of-bundled-p (archived at https://perma.cc/AJB7-DNTD) [accessed 03 April 2018]

18 Hester, J (2015) The tyranny of freebies, *CityLab*, 05 June [online] www.citylab.com/life/2015/06/psychology-of-free-donuts/395021/ (archived at https://perma.cc/Q9W9-AZ5L) [accessed 01 May 2018]

19 DeMers, J (2016) 5 ways to increase sales using the psychology of pricing, *Forbes*, 03 May [online] www.forbes.com/sites/jaysondemers/2016/05/03/5-ways-to-increase-sales-using-the-psychology-of-pricing/2/#486b3e921c90 (archived at https://perma.cc/8ASF-WWY7) [accessed 05 April 2018]

20 McRaney, D (2011) *You Are Not So Smart: Why you have too many friends on Facebook, why your memory is mostly fiction, and 46 other ways you're deluding yourself*, Penguin, New York

21 Ariel, Dr A (2010) *Predictably Irrational, revised and expanded edition: The hidden forces that shape our decisions*, HarperCollins, New York

22 Thomas, M and Morwitz, V (2005) Penny wise and pound foolish: the left-digit effect in price cognition, *Journal of Consumer Research* [online] https://academic.oup.com/jcr/article-abstract/32/1/54/1796360 (archived at https://perma.cc/3GVZ-LTK3) [accessed 05 April 2018]

23 Simester, D I and Anderson E T (2003) Effects of $9 price endings on retail sales: evidence from field experiments, *Semantic Scholar* [online] pdfs.semanticscholar.org/ee6b/d0c4e357f043a51618a672b-f7d0f15df8825.pdf (archived at https://perma.cc/D4KK-MKQT) [accessed 05 April 2018]

24 Poundstone, W (2011) *Priceless: The myth of fair value (and how to take advantage of it*, Hill and Wang, New York

25 Business Dictionary (nd) Prestige pricing, definition [online] www.businessdictionary.com/definition/prestige-pricing.html (archived at https://perma.cc/NN2B-MCWK) [accessed 05 April 2018]

26 Wadhwa, M and Zhang, K (2015) This number just feels right: the impact of roundedness of price numbers on product evaluations, *Journal of Consumer Research*, 01 February [online] academic.oup.com/jcr/article-abstract/41/5/1172/2962090?redirectedFrom=fulltext (archived at https://perma.cc/T7X6-W74X) [accessed 05 April 2018]

THE PURPOSE OF A BRAND
IS TO BUILD AWARENESS

Brand awareness refers to the extent to which a brand is known within its marketplace. There are two different types of awareness: brand recognition is the ability of a person to recognize a brand when they are in its proximity; brand recall is when an individual can remember a brand, unaided, while thinking of a particular category of goods or services.

Brand recognition is most important when customers face a choice. For example, when walking around the supermarket, customers will see brands that they recognize in a particular category, eg toothpaste or laundry detergent. In this scenario they will most likely gravitate to the products with which they are familiar. Similarly, when searching online for a particular product or service, people are inclined to click on the links of companies they've heard of.

Brand recall is important when there is no selection in front of a customer. For instance, a person may offer to go out and buy snacks for the rest of their colleagues in the office. One individual may ask for a Snickers bar: this is brand recall. The ultimate in brand recall is having 'top of mind awareness'. This refers to the first brand that a person recollects in a particular category [1]. So, on wanting to buy a pair of trainers, a purchaser may go straight onto the Nike website as it is the first brand that comes to mind.

Awareness is a prerequisite to purchase. If people don't know that a company, brand or product exists, then they cannot buy. Any offering must generate awareness whether it is a brand or not, otherwise it will fail. However, although vital, awareness is not the reason a brand is created.

Interestingly, the concept of 'branding' has been around a long time. The Ancient Egyptians used it in order to differentiate one person's cattle from another's [2]. A distinctive symbol was burned onto the animal's skin [3]. In fact, the English word 'brand' comes from the Norse word *brandr*, which referred to burning the symbol on animals as practised by cattle owners in Scandinavia [4].

So, as we can see historically, the first function of a brand is to distinguish one offering from another. While this worked for cattle owners as a form of identification, a simple symbol, name or logo would not enable a customer to distinguish between offerings.

For instance, two similar jars of strawberry jam could be next to each other. There could be a different, insignificant symbol on each lid, neither of which convey anything. Technically, it would be possible to distinguish between them because they look different. However, this distinction would be inconsequential, because the difference wouldn't provide any further meaningful information that may influence a purchase.

In order for a symbol, name or logo to have significance, from a customer perspective it has to provide meaning. Of course, a symbol, name or logo could create meaning by implying something about the offering. A jam using a big smiley face as a logo might infer that it makes people happy, even if you have not heard of the brand before.

When branding was first used to sell goods, it did indeed provide some useful distinctions between offerings. Merchandise such as precious metals, textiles, pottery, oils and wines were often given specific marks to show the origin of the materials. It was also a form of quality control [5].

In the Middle Ages, merchants' guilds throughout Europe used marks as a quality guarantee and to prevent the counterfeiting of goods [6]. There are labels today that work in this way. For example, any drink designated as Scotch immediately lets a purchaser know that the whisky has been produced from a distillery in Scotland using water and malted barley [7]. As Scotland has a good reputation for producing whisky, a certain quality is inferred by this identity.

Branding historically achieved two outcomes: 1) it allowed companies and purchasers to distinguish between products; 2) brands were also marks of trust providing information about the origin and quality of the goods. Of course, today, branding still achieves these results. One of the reasons consumers are often willing to pay more for a brand is that it lowers the risk of purchase [8]. A known brand provides reassurance that the buyer will obtain the outcome they desire.

Modern branding, as we understand it today, started to develop in the second half of the 19th century [9]. Before this time, manufacturers of products were unknown to purchasers who relied on their local retailer [10]. The Industrial Revolution enabled the mass production of goods as well as better transportation, providing businesses with the opportunity to scale and sell their goods to a greater number of customers. As products became more available, it became increasingly important for manufacturers to distinguish their offerings.

Companies started to use distinctive packaging, as well as emotional and memorable associations in their advertising, in order to sell their goods. Early examples of this are Quaker Oats which, in 1877, was the first trademark for a breakfast cereal [11]. The trademark was a figure of a man in Quaker clothing, both personalizing the cereal and associating it with characteristics such as quality and honesty.

During the 1920s, Edward Bernays wrote a number of articles culminating in his 1928 book *Propaganda* [12]. It should be noted that propaganda became associated with a negative meaning when it was used so effectively by the Nazi regime in Germany, but in

1928 this was not the case [13]. In his book, Bernays suggested that by linking products with ideas, people could be persuaded to change their behaviour.

This idea was expanded upon in another of Bernays' books, *The Engineering of Consent*, published in 1955 [14]. The book expressed the view that human motivations and inner desires lay within a person's subconscious. By understanding these desires, companies could improve their sales strategy. This concept was extremely influential and certainly impacted marketing and communications professionals [13]. Today we are used to brands having an emotional proposition – whether it's Volvo signifying safety [15], Disney providing magic [16] or Nike enhancing performance [17].

On 13 May 1931, Neil McElroy, working at Procter & Gamble, sent a memo to his boss justifying why he needed to hire two more people in the promotions department. The memo is widely credited as creating the discipline of brand management [18], whereby a brand manager leads a team to manage the success of a product. This is instead of positions being based on business function, which had traditionally been the case. These ideas were subsequently copied by many other businesses [19].

The economic boom after World War II, together with the golden age of television, led to the brand building with which we are now familiar. An increase in customer choice combined with the ability for brands to reach extremely large audiences, led to more sophistication in the way they communicated.

In 1955, Burleigh Gardner and Sidney Levy wrote a seminal article in the *Harvard Business Review* articulating the idea of Brand Image [20]. In a world where many brands were making similar claims, they sighted the importance of a 'governing product and brand personality that is unified and coherently meaningful' [21]. This idea was quickly utilized by many individuals including David Ogilvy, one of the most important figures in advertising, who picked up on their recommendation for 'long-term investment in the personality of the brand' [22].

By understanding the evolution of branding, we can recognize that functionally, branding has three objectives. First, it distinguishes one product or service from another. Second, it is a trust mark providing the consumer with reassurance about the quality of the offering. Third, it creates a personality for something that is inanimate, giving it life, establishing an emotional link with the audience and thus making it more desirable.

A customer has to be aware of a brand for it to achieve any of these specific objectives. Awareness, however, is not one of the aims in itself. Of course, all of this should increase sales, which is ultimately what any commercial enterprise is trying to achieve.

Interestingly, it is through looking at branding from a consumer perspective that the real power of a brand can be appreciated. Today, in most product or service categories, customers are overwhelmed with choice. Many of the costs of purchase are cognitive; that is, the time that needs to be put into research, thinking and choosing. Of course, people will exert themselves to reduce the risk of purchase. For example, an individual is likely to spend more time choosing a house or car than selecting toilet paper, as the risks of making a mistake are considerably different.

However, cognitive economy tells us that the information processing capacity of any purchaser is finite [23]. This results in customers often choosing offerings that are easier to purchase, rather than the ones that might be absolutely best for their objectives [24]. For example, when shopping in a supermarket and being overwhelmed by the number of different soup options on the shelves, shoppers will often reach for the brands they know, such as Campbell's or Heinz. Similarly, if looking for a car, a purchaser may start out with a few selected brands with which they are familiar.

In other words, brands do not exist to build awareness, although like any offer, they cannot be effective without customers being aware of them. In a world where we have an abundance of choice, and insufficient time, brands are a short-cut to ensuring that when making a purchase, a customer obtains something on which they can rely, and which will meet their requirements. Put simply, what brands ultimately achieve is to make it easier for customers to buy.

Notes

1 Hendricks, B (nd) Top of mind awareness: definition & theory [online] study.com/academy/lesson/top-of-mind-awareness-definition-theory.html (archived at https://perma.cc/X6RX-GNQ8) [accessed 08 April 2018]

2 Wheeler, H (1946) *The Miracle Of Man,* Longacre, London

3 Academy of IRMBR (2017) International research in management & business realities, *Brand Marketing and Consumer Behavior* [online] www.academyirmbr.com/special.php (archived at https://perma.cc/TB5H-4VWA) [accessed 16 April 2018]

4 Keller, Dr K L, Apéria, T and Georgson, M (2008) *Strategic Brand Management: A European perspective*, Pearson Education, Harlow

5 Cartwright, M (2013) Trade in the Roman World, *Ancient History Encyclopedia,* 17 December [online] www.ancient.eu/article/638/trade-in-the-roman-world/ (archived at https://perma.cc/HNJ6-PLTG) [accessed 09 April 2018]

6 Brian Jones, D G and Tadajewski, M (2016) *The Routledge Companion to Marketing History*, Routledge, London and New York

7 Scotch Whisky Association (2009) The Scotch Whisky Regulations [online] https://www.scotch-whisky.org.uk/media/1360/scotchwhiskyregguidance2009-amended.pdf (archived at https://perma.cc/4SDU-5967) [accessed 10 April 2018]

8 Erdem, T, Swait, J D and Louviere, J (2002) The impact of brand credibility on consumer price sensitivity, *International Journal of Research in Marketing* [online] pdfs.semanticscholar.org/332f/3b19ca2dc5c7cb7e12c2f17458f2b39f19cf.pdf (archived at https://perma.cc/7SZJ-6PAX) [accessed 11 April 2018]

9 Klein, N (2009) *No Logo: Taking Aim at the Brand Bullies,* Picador, New York

10 AdAge (2003) History: 19th century, *AdAge,* 15 September [online] adage.com (archived at https://perma.cc/R32Y-7AXV) [accessed 12 April 2018]

11 QuakerOat (nd) Our Oat Origins [online] www.quakeroats.com/about-quaker-oats/content/quaker-history.aspx (archived at https://perma.cc/L9ZM-27SL) [accessed 12 April 2018]

12 Bernays, E (1928) *Propaganda*, Ig Publishing, New York

13 Gunderman, R (2015) The manipulation of the American mind: Edward Bernays and the birth of public relations, *The Conversation*, 09 July [online] theconversation.com/the-manipulation-of-the-american-mind-edward-bernays-and-the-birth-of-public-relations-44393 (archived at https://perma.cc/SU77-4XJA) [accessed 12 April 2018]

14 Bernays, E (1955) *The Engineering of Consent*, Norman, University of Oklahoma Press

15 Volvo Car Group (2003) Safety: the sights are set on leadership [online] www.media.volvocars.com/global/en-gb/media/pressreleases/5252 (archived at https://perma.cc/845Q-CZZ7) [accessed 02 May 2018]

16 Adamson, A (2014) Disney knows it's not just magic that keeps a brand on top, *Forbes*, 15 October [online] www.forbes.com/sites/allenadamson/2014/10/15/disney-knows-its-not-just-magic-that-keeps-a-brand-on-top/#1ac7dbef5b26 (archived at https://perma.cc/HB4G-RBQL) [accessed 02 May 2018]

17 Ford, E (2016) 5 luxury branding lessons from Nike, *The Sports Marketing Playbook*, 24 January [online] thesportsmarketingplaybook.com/2016/01/24/5-luxury-branding-lessons-from-nike/ (archived at https://perma.cc/9VX8-LMQ9) [accessed 02 May 2018]

18 Daye, D (2009) Great moments in branding: Neil McElroy memo, *Brand Strategy Insider*, 12 June [online] www.brandingstrategyinsider.com/2009/06/great-moments-in-branding-neil-mcelroy-memo.html#.WtBru9Nubwc (archived at https://perma.cc/T4ZK-STJ3) [accessed 13 April 2018]

19 Ritson, M (2009) Mark Ritson on branding: a memo to end all memos, *Campaign*, 11 May [online] www.campaignlive.co.uk/article/mark-ritson-branding-memo-end-memos/904997 (archived at https://perma.cc/WUV6-M2D3) [accessed 14 April 2018]

20 Gardner, B B and Levy, S J (1955) The product and the brand, *Harvard Business Review* [online] static.squarespace.com/static/52f06caee4b0c058f6084354/t/539070a1e4b0b438 0bb48719/1401974945820/Levy_ProductandBrand.pdf (archived at https://perma.cc/D9WE-EDR2) [accessed 15 April 2018]

21 Levy, S J (1999) Brands, consumers, symbols and research, in *Sidney J Levy on Marketing*, Sage Publications, London

22 Ogilvy (nd) Our History [online] www.ogilvy.com/our-history/ (archived at https://perma.cc/J8RH-QZUN) [accessed 15 April 2018]

23 Martens, B (2004) *The Cognitive Mechanics of Economic Development and Institutional Change*, Routledge, London

24 Dawar, N (2013) *Tilt: Shifting your strategy from products to customers*, Harvard Business School Publishing, Boston

**MYTH
10**

EVERY BUSINESS IS A BRAND

The UK's Chartered Institute of Marketing defines brand as 'The set of physical attributes of a product or service, together with the beliefs and expectations surrounding it – a unique combination which the name or logo of the product or service should evoke in the mind of the audience' [1].

Unpacking this definition makes it easy to understand the different aspects of a brand. There are physical attributes; this can be the look and feel of a product itself, such as the VW Beetle. It can also be the packaging; think of the Coca-Cola glass bottle. Physical attributes also include the tangible benefits one expects to receive from the offering. For example, the UK's Premier Inn Hotels offer a good night sleep guarantee. If you don't get a good night sleep, you get your money back [2].

The beliefs and expectations are the values, emotions and feelings that a brand evokes. For instance, even the name suggests that the smoothies and other products that Innocent Drinks produce won't harm you. Their website states that to make their smoothies they use the finest fruit they can find and never add sugar or colourings [3]. When they were founded in 1999, they declared their mission was 'to help make it easier for people to do themselves some good'. They state that what they provide is 'natural delicious drinks that help people live well and die old' [4].

Another example of brand beliefs is Dove's mission 'to ensure that the next generation grows up enjoying a positive relationship with the way they look – helping young people raise their self-esteem and realize their full potential' [5]. In line with this mission statement, the aim of the Dove 'Real Beauty' campaign is to celebrate all different types of women and challenge the traditional media stereotype of who is beautiful [6].

There are many brands that have used pure emotion and feelings in their communications. Procter & Gamble's 'Thank you Mum' campaign was a poignant and sensitive reminder, for both parents and children, of the pivotal role that mothers play in our lives [7]. Of course, underlying the message is the essential part that Procter & Gamble's products play in the life of a mum. Nappies such as Pampers, washing detergent like Tide and toothpaste, for example Crest, are all household necessities.

The use of emotions and feelings is not exclusive to business-to-consumer communications. Cisco Systems is a good example of a business-to-business brand that has used emotion to solidify its position as a market leader. For example, watch Cisco's 2014 Internet of Everything commercial, which uses a narrative of a little girl giving her cat milk to demonstrate how technology is changing the world, while positioning Cisco at the heart of that change [8].

It is the blend of both the 'physical attributes of a product or service, combined with the beliefs and expectations surrounding it' that should be unique. In other words, it isn't just what a company does, or how it does it, but also the values and emotions with which it is associated that collectively create an offering that is different from others in the market.

Apple are not the only company to make media devices, Rolex are not the sole manufacturer of luxury watches, and McKinsey & Company are not the only management consultants in the world. It is the combination of their physical attributes and the way they are delivered, together with the beliefs and expectations connected with these brands that gives each of them a unique identity.

Finally, it is the name, the logo, or both, that should be recognized and immediately evoke particular attributes, beliefs and expectations. The golden arches of McDonald's, the Nike swoosh and the letters IBM all immediately stand for something when seen or heard by consumers.

The common misconception is that because almost every business has a name, and many have a logo, this automatically means that they have a brand. However, a brand is only a brand if the name or logo has meaning; in other words, if it evokes certain expectations, emotions and feelings with the target audience. For many small and medium-sized businesses this simply isn't the case. The name and logo mean nothing, even to their target market.

An overwhelming majority of the small and medium-sized businesses that I have met have never strategically thought about the emotions and feelings they want their company to convey. Sure, almost all of them want to do business with integrity and serve the customer well, but they have not carved out a unique position for themselves in the market by fostering an emotional connection between their offering and the customer.

The name of their business and logo evoke no feelings or expectations in the minds of their prospects. When many of these businesses are liked, trusted and respected it is the individual owner of the company who creates these perceptions, rather than the branding of the company itself.

This has led many individuals to talk about 'personal branding', an idea widely attributed to an article in *Fast Company* magazine written by Tom Peters in 1997 [9]. However, I would argue that the concept of 'personal branding' is utterly ridiculous.

Branding is the process of taking an inanimate, indistinguishable product or service and making it distinctive and meaningful. By definition, every individual is unique. No human being has to go through a branding process to make them original or differentiate them from others. Therefore, the idea of branding a human being is an oxymoron.

It is of course true that the way people think about, and perceive, an individual will affect their career, achievements and, if they are the owner of a business, the success of their company. All of us today are public figures because of social media. People can look at our LinkedIn, Twitter and Facebook profiles and make judgements, even before any personal interaction has taken place.

But this phenomenon should not be confused with 'brand'. This is 'reputation'. People will then cite individuals such as Michael Jordan, Oprah Winfrey or Lady Gaga as people with great 'personal brands'. Actually, they are popular because they possess talents which other people enjoy, admire or to which they aspire. They did not go through any branding exercise in order to make them distinctive. They are extraordinary.

Of course, they will have consultants assisting them with their visual image as well as public relations specialists advising them on what to say and what not to say. This is in order to enhance or maintain their reputation. The essence of what makes them special, their talent, personality and abilities, were not created by branding consultants.

Every individual has a reputation which they need to manage carefully as it will affect their success. The difference between high-profile celebrities and the rest of us is scale. Many owners of successful small and medium-sized companies are held in high regard. It is not the company brand that leads people to do business with the enterprise but the leader's reputation.

Whether a business requires a brand or not very much depends on the ambition of the enterprise. Individuals running small businesses such as electricians, plumbers, gardeners and builders, with no appetite to scale and grow, probably do not require a brand. Of course, what they do need is a good reputation. The same is likely to be true of small accountancy practices, law firms and other service providers where it is the senior individuals in the business who attract customers through personal recommendations, interactions and their own reputation. Once a company wants to scale, in order to serve a much wider audience or be sustainable beyond a few key individuals, it will then need to create a brand.

It should be noted that there are companies that have both a well-known individual leading the business as well as a brand. Steve Jobs was synonymous with the success of Apple although, because it has a brand, it has still been prosperous many years after he passed away [10]. Similarly, Bill Gates stepped down as the CEO of Microsoft in 2000, yet it still continues to function as a business [11].

Creating a brand requires a strategy where the ethos, value proposition, identity, personality, emotions and feelings of the organization are defined. An investment will then be required in order to communicate these messages both internally within the organization, as well as externally to the target market. Without this strategic thinking and investment, it is unlikely a company will ever have a brand. There are many profitable small businesses run by successful individuals with good reputations. Many of these companies will not have a brand, nor do they necessarily require one. An organization does not have a brand merely by being in business.

Notes

1 CIM (nd) Marketing Expert [online] marketingexpert.cim.co.uk/glossary/ (archived at https://perma.cc/MM9U-7DZE) [accessed 18 April 2018]

2 Premiere Inn (nd) Good Night Guarantee [online] www.premierinn.com/gb/en/why/sleep/good-night-guarantee.html (archived at https://perma.cc/23S3-VAYW) [accessed 18 April 2018]

3 Innocentdrinks (nd) Smoothies [online] www.innocentdrinks.co.uk/things-we-make (archived at https://perma.cc/U67T-CAZK) [accessed 20 April 2018]

4 Innocentdrinks (nd) Our story: Hello, we're innocent [online] www.innocentdrinks.co.uk/us/our-story (archived at https://perma.cc/XM8Z-ZUXW) [accessed 20 April 2018]

5 Dove website (nd) Our mission [Online] www.dove.com/in/dove-self-esteem-project/our-mission.html (archived at https://perma.cc/6RFW-ZNPW) [accessed 25 April 2018]

6 Dove (nd) Be Real: the campaign for body confidence [online] www.dove.com/in/dove-self-esteem-project/help-for-parents/talking-about-appearance/be-real-the-campaign-for-body-confidence.html (archived at https://perma.cc/DZK4-HFVK) [accessed 25 April 2018]

7 P&G (2017) Procter & Gamble launches global 'Thank You Mom' campaign for London 2012 Olympic Games planning to raise $5 million for youth sports and support more than 150 athletes [online] news.pg.com/press-release/pg-corporate-announcements/procter-gamble-launches-global-thank-you-mom-campaign-londo (archived at https://perma.cc/4UW8-P25P) [accessed 25 April 2018]

8 Cisco (2014) Internet of Everything Commercial by Cisco Commercial 2014 [online] https://www.youtube.com/watch?v=5Jxo7AGZmMw (archived at https://perma.cc/GZ9Y-JX2L) [accessed 25 April 2018]

9 Peters, T (1997) The brand called you, *Fast Company*, 31 August [online] www.fastcompany.com/28905/brand-called-you (archived at https://perma.cc/3BJC-MUL7) [accessed 26 April 2018]

10 Snell, J (2018) 5 takeaways from Apple's record second-quarter 2018 results, *Macworld*, 01 May [online] www.macworld.com/article/3269608/techology-business/5-takeaways-from-apples-record-second-quarter-2018-results.html (archived at https://perma.cc/6U9J-R33L) [accessed 03 May 2018]

11 Reuters (2017) Strong profits gives Microsoft's stock a big lift, *Fortune*, 26 October [online] fortune.com/2017/10/26/microsoft-stock-big-lift/ (archived at https://perma.cc/4CWJ-ASEJ) [accessed 03 May 2018]

BUSINESS-TO-BUSINESS PURCHASES ARE PURELY BASED ON LOGIC

Whether it is Nike's 'Find Your Greatness' campaign, telling us that greatness is in everyone [1], UPS's message concerning delivering wishes, with the spotlight on a four-year-old boy called Carson [2], or the Budweiser commercial that focused on the friendship between a puppy and a Clydesdale horse [3], as consumers we are used to seeing communications that concentrate on feelings and emotions. Many of these promotions offer no rational benefits or justifications for the innumerable products and services that we purchase, or brand preferences upon which we decide.

We tend to accept that these emotional messages are effective in business-to-consumer marcom, but there is a commonly held view that when it comes to business-to-business purchases, people buy purely on logic or reason [4]. What this assumption doesn't take into account is that while the circumstances may be different, human beings don't fundamentally change simply because they are in a business environment.

This was recognized by Herbert Simon, whose theory of 'bounded rationality' makes the argument that it is impossible for individuals to arrive at any truly rational decision, in any scenario, because of three missing criteria. He explained: 'Firstly, the decision maker would need knowledge of all the possible alternatives. Secondly, they would have to understand the consequences of each of these alternatives. Finally, they would have to be able to predict the relative value of each of these different consequences' [5].

Not only do human beings lack all the necessary information, but Simon also questioned the cognitive ability of human beings to process it all if they did have it. He goes on: 'The capacity of the human mind for formulating and solving complex problems is very small compared with the size of the problems whose solution is required for objectively rational behaviour in the real world – or even for a reasonable approximation to such objective rationality' [6]. Simon proposed that rather than trying to achieve the optimum result, decision makers would attempt to obtain an outcome that was good enough, or 'satisficing' – a word he coined which blends satisfy and suffice [7]. While obtaining the optimum result may be impossible, Simon believed an individual could achieve a 'satisficing' outcome by making decisions using relatively simple heuristics or rules of thumb [8].

It is this use of heuristics, as pointed out by Simon, that Amos Tversky and Daniel Kahneman, in their 1974 paper 'Judgement under Uncertainty', highlighted can lead to cognitive biases. They explained that, 'People rely on a limited number of heuristic principles which reduce the complex tasks of assessing probabilities and predicting values to simpler judgemental operations. In general, these heuristics are quite useful, but sometimes they lead to severe and systematic errors' [9]. These can push people to make unreliable judgements. This demonstrated how human beings are not purely rational actors. Daniel Kahneman shared many of his findings in his 2011 book, *Thinking, Fast and Slow* [10]. In this volume, Kahneman explains how human beings have two modes of thinking: System 1 and System 2.

System 1 thinking is fast, instinctive and subconscious whereas System 2 is slower, reasoned, conscious and effortful [11]. What's significant to note, Kahneman points out, is that most decisions are made by System 1: 'Thinking is to humans as swimming is to cats; they can do it, but they would prefer not to' [12]. More often than not, the conscious mind merely post-rationalizes decisions that have already been made. This gives us the impression that most of our judgements are logical and reasoned when they are not. As the social psychologist Jonathan Haidt explains, 'The rational mind thinks of itself as the Oval Office when actually it's the press office' [13].

So how does this apply to consumers? Harvard Business School professor Gerald Zaltman states that 95 per cent of our purchase decision making takes place in the subconscious mind [14]. This makes emotion vital. It is not that the subconscious mind is itself emotional, but rather emotion is the way that the subconscious communicates with the conscious mind. These findings are borne out by the work of neuroscientist Antonio Damasio. His 'Somatic Marker Hypothesis' demonstrates that people need emotional reactions in order to make sound decisions [15]. In his 1994 book *Descartes' Error*, Damasio showed how people with a high level of reasoning, but with an impaired ability to process emotion, struggled to make decisions [16]. As Damasio puts it himself, 'We are not thinking machines. We are feeling machines that think' [17].

The way human beings cognitively process and make sense of information does not change simply because one is in a corporate setting. If the subconscious mind, through the emotions evoked, is the primary driver in reaching decisions, this is the case for business-to-business purchases as well as in business-to-consumer buying. For an enterprise to ignore the emotional element when buyers are procuring a product or service is to disregard the dominant consideration affecting the outcome.

In fact, one could argue that emotional determinants are now playing an even greater part in business-to-business purchasing. In the current B2B climate, buying criteria has become more robust; procurement teams now rationalize and quantify all elements of an acquisition. Meeting a buyer's vigorous demands is now a minimum requirement to even be considered as a supplier, so companies increasingly find the procurement process results in their offerings being commoditized. This lack of differentiation merely heightens the importance of emotional considerations in any buying decision [18].

In an article for the *Harvard Business Review* entitled 'The B2B Elements of Value', authors Eric Almquist, Jamie Cleghorn and Lori Sherer point out that as well as the expected logical and quantifiable criteria of purchase, emotional considerations such as whether the product can enhance the buyer's reputation or reduce their anxiety are playing a role in the decision-making process [18]. In the battle for differentiation they observe that subjective emotional considerations, such as cultural fit and the seller's commitment to the customer, are becoming more important.

And it is not just the emotional considerations that affect the business at large that are being taken into account. A study by the Corporate Executive Board (now Gartner), in partnership with Google, showed that personal value such as career advancement, popularity, confidence and pride had twice as much impact on purchasers than business value. Moreover, the study demonstrated that buyers were over seven times more likely to pay a premium for comparable offerings when personal value is present [19].

This research also revealed that a greater proportion of business-to-business customers are emotionally attached to a company they purchased from when compared with business-to-consumer buyers [19]. Emotionally, they have more vested in the purchase because the risks of failure are far higher. Downsides such as bad business performance, financial losses or the damage to personal reputation are potentially far more harmful than the ramifications of most personal purchasing. These findings are supported by Daniel Kahneman and Amos Tversky's 'Prospect Theory', which found that people are much more mindful and sensitive to potential losses than to likely gains [20].

These personal emotional considerations are valid whether the business decision is being taken by one person, within a company, or by a decision-making unit with a number of personnel. Back in the 1960s, Nobel Prize-winning economist Oliver E Williamson, with his model of 'Managerial Discretion', demonstrated how people balance their personal priorities with maximizing the profits of the company for which they are working [21].

Armed with this understanding of the way that human beings cognitively make judgements, it's clear that emotion is just as important in business-to-business purchasing as in that of business-to-consumer. Moreover, personal considerations do have an influence on what would seem to be a purely business decision. These personal factors hold even more sway when there is a lack of differentiation between offerings. All these elements, together with our heightened aversion to risk and the greater potential for failure in a business-to-business setting, makes emotion and feelings fundamental components in business-to-business purchase decisions.

Just as in business-to-consumer marketing, organizations in the business-to-business domain need to identify and communicate their emotional selling proposition to their customers. Equally, mechanisms such as the power of stories, which can impart real information while providing emotion and evoking feelings, are plainly as essential for companies in business as they are for consumer offerings. The power of a respected brand, which gives emotional meaning to a product or service as well as minimizing the perceived risk involved, is as important in the business-to-business world as in the area of business-to-consumer marketing. To ignore feelings and emotion, simply because one is selling to businesses rather than consumers, is to render any marcom efforts far less effective than they would be otherwise.

Notes

1 Nike (2012) Find Your Greatness [online] https://www.youtube.com (archived at https://perma.cc/6GB3-43S4) [accessed 22 May 2018]

2 UPS (2014) Your Wishes Delivered: Driver for a Day [online] www.youtube.com (archived at https://perma.cc/XL5E-NZWH) [accessed 22 May 2018]

3 Budweiser (2014) Budweiser USA: Super Bowl XLVIII Commercial, 'Puppy Love' – Telling the Story [online] www.youtube.com (archived at https://perma.cc/XL5E-NZWH) [accessed 22 May 2018]

4 Andersson, J, Kaplar, E and Selö, N (2013) Functional or emotional values in B2B? A study of marketing communication in the B2B healthcare market, Halmstad University, 21 May [online] www.diva-portal.org/smash/get/diva2:629469/FULLTEXT01.pdf (archived at https://perma.cc/HS85-8W5T) [accessed 22 May 2018]

5 Barros, G (2010) Herbert A. Simon and the concept of rationality: boundaries and procedures, *Brazilian Journal of Political Economy* [Online] www.scielo.br/scielo.php?script=sci_arttext&pid=S0101-31572010000300006 (archived at https://perma.cc/Y3QP-D67H) [accessed 22 May 2018]

6 Simon, H (1957) *Models of Man: Social and rational. Mathematical essays on rational human behavior in a social setting*, Wiley, New York

7 Wikipedia (nd) Satisficing, *Wikipedia* [online] en.wikipedia.org/wiki/Satisficing (archived at https://perma.cc/T3S2-3JA6) [accessed 22 May 2018]

8 Fox, J (2014) When a simple rule of thumb beats a fancy algorithm, *Harvard Business Review*, 02 October [online] hbr.org/2014/10/when-a-simple-rule-of-thumb-beats-a-fancy-algorithm (archived at https://perma.cc/W2F8-L8S8) [accessed 31 May 2018]

9 Tversky, A and Kahneman, D (1974) Judgment under uncertainty: heuristics and biases, *Science* [Online] https://science.sciencemag.org/content/185/4157/1124 (archived at https://perma.cc/6FG5-2RZH) [accessed 22 May 2018]

10 Kahneman, D (2011) *Thinking, Fast and Slow*, Farrar, Straus and Giroux, New York

11 Ipsos Encyclopedia (2017) System 1/ System 2 [online] www.ipsos.com/en/ipsos-encyclopedia-system-1-system-2 (archived at https://perma.cc/YYE5-PQBJ) [accessed 04 June 2018]

12 Shotton, R (2014) Fast and slow lessons for marketers, *Guardian*, 07 April [online] www.theguardian.com/media-network/media-network-blog/2014/apr/07/thinking-fast-slow-marketers-consumers (archived at https://perma.cc/AG2J-XRVQ) [accessed 22 May 2018]

13 Shotton, R (2018) *The Choice Factory: 25 behavioural biases that influence what we buy*, Harriman House, Petersfield

14 Mahony, M (2003) The subconscious mind of the consumer (and how to reach it), *Harvard Business School*, 13 January [online] hbswk.hbs.edu/item/the-subconscious-mind-of-the-consumer-and-how-to-reach-it (archived at https://perma.cc/H77A-8YB7) [accessed 22 May 2018]

15 Pauen, M (2006) Emotion, decision, and mental models, *Advances in Psychology* [online] www.sciencedirect.com/topics/neuroscience/somatic-marker-hypothesis [accessed 22 May 2018]

16 Graves, C (2015) Part One: 'We are not thinking machines. We are feeling machines that think', *Institute for PR*, 17 March [online] instituteforpr.org/part-one-not-thinking-machines-feeling-machines-think/ (archived at https://perma.cc/LG4M-C2QB) [accessed 22 May 2018]

17 Damasio, A (2005) *Descartes' Error: Emotion, reason, and the human brain*, HarperCollins, New York

18 Almquist, E, Cleghorn, J and Sherer, L (2018) The B2B elements of value, *Harvard Business Review*, March [online] hbr.org/2018/03/the-b2b-elements-of-value (archived at https://perma.cc/JWC6-APT4) [accessed 22 May 2018]

19 Zhang, J, Bird, A and Leroy, A (2013) From promotion to emotion, connecting B2B customers to brands, *CEB Marketing Leadership Council* [online] www.cebglobal.com/content/dam/cebglobal/us/EN/best-practices-decision-support/marketing-communications/pdfs/promotion-emotion-whitepaper-full.pdf (archived at https://perma.cc/MNQ7-9U4T) [accessed 22 May 2018]

20 Kahneman, D and Tversky, A (1979) Prospect Theory, An analysis of decision under risk, *Econonometrica*, March [online] people.hss.caltech.edu/~camerer/Ec101/ProspectTheory.pdf (archived at https://perma.cc/83XM-RZHP) [accessed 04 June 2018]

21 Economics Discussion (nd) 'Williamson's Model of Managerial' Available from: www.economicsdiscussion.net/firm/williamsons-model-of-managerial-discretion/5718 (archived at https://perma.cc/82TV-CR52) [accessed 22 May 2018]

BUSINESS-TO-BUSINESS AND BUSINESS-TO-CONSUMER MARKETING ARE COMPLETELY DIFFERENT

There is a widely held view that marketing in business-to-business (B2B) is completely different from business-to-consumer (B2C). While many corporations focus on one or the other, there are examples of companies that service both groups. Airlines such as British Airways, technology companies like Apple and telecommunications providers such as Verizon in the United States, have offerings for both the business and domestic markets.

Regardless of the audience, marketing is 'the process of determining, communicating and delivering value in order to obtain and retain customers'. This objective is the same whether the buyers are corporations or households. Furthermore, the 'marketing mix', as we defined it in Myth 2, using the acronym CAVE, is relevant in both cases.

Companies have to 'Communicate' with their prospects. They must decide how their products and services will be 'Accessed' and the different contacts and touchpoints that will be established. The price and cost of purchase, ownership and implementation must be considered in order to ensure that a buyer identifies 'Value' in the offer. The whole 'Experience', from the product or service itself, to any support, interactions and customer involvement must be evaluated to ensure that an organization's offering is compelling. These factors must be decided whether or not one is operating in a B2B or B2C environment.

Other core marketing disciplines such as the sufficient measurement of activities, the effective use of data, ensuring that the business is truly customer focused and the understanding of the buying journey, are relevant for both B2B and B2C marketers. Of course, purchase journeys in the B2B world are often different from those in B2C. B2B organizations tend to have formal processes which can result in the acquisition taking longer [1]. This may require a greater degree of lead nurturing from a marketing department and an understanding of the distinct stages that lead to a sale. Although applied differently, the understanding of the buying journey is relevant in both B2B and B2C marketing.

Similarly, B2B purchases often include a greater number of influencers and decision makers than in B2C [1]. This may require a marketing department to have complimentary, and yet distinctive, messaging for the various buyers. In many ways, this is no different from a B2C offering that appeals to a number of specific types of consumer.

The further it is explored the more apparent it is that there are an overwhelming number of similarities between the B2B and B2C worlds of marketing. For example, both must ensure they understand the marketplace in which they are operating and deliberate factors such as market trends, competitors and changing customer requirements.

Proponents of the differences between B2B and B2C will point out that many of these marketing disciplines are applied differently. So, while market segmentation must be undertaken by any enterprise to ensure its relevance, target markets for B2B providers tend to be smaller. These types of generalizations, however, rarely stand up to scrutiny. For example, an independent restaurant, hair salon or bar, servicing a local community, has a relatively small target market compared with B2B enterprises such as Oracle, McKinsey or SAP.

Buyer motivations are another factor highlighted as different between B2B purchasers and consumers. It is often asserted that in business, purchases are undertaken when they are deemed essential, whereas consumers have more of a tendency to buy products and services that they want, and when no absolute requirement is necessary.

In reality, it depends on the particular offering a company provides. For example, there are plenty of B2C purchases that are deemed as essential requirements including utilities, insurance, food, housing etc – the list goes on. Even items such as cars, which for some buyers might be an exciting discretionary lifestyle purchase, for others will be seen as an absolute requirement due to their living circumstances.

Similarly, while in business there will be many acquisitions that are deemed essential, there will be others that are more open to choice. Purchases relating to a big end-of-year company party, a new swanky office fit-out, business-class travel for all senior management and team-building away days are not usually regarded as absolute imperatives.

The fact is that many of the distinctions made between B2B and B2C are more about the category the acquisition falls into, rather than whether it is a business or consumer purchase. For example, the customer journey for buying life insurance is completely different from that of toothpaste, but both are consumer offerings. Meanwhile, a company will not utilize the same group of C-Suite decision makers to choose a new water cooler supplier for a regional office, as it would to purchase Enterprise Resource Planning (ERP) software across the entire global business.

It becomes obvious when considering these examples that thinking of the differences in marketing by the category of offering, rather than a general B2B and B2C split, is more helpful. For example, it is argued that in B2B more detailed product and service information is required. It will, though, depend on what a company is selling. I doubt if the office manager purchasing stationery is looking for granular details about the packet of whiteboard markers for which they have been asked. Meanwhile, a consumer may want to understand the finer details of the health insurance policy that they intend buying.

Probably the biggest perceived difference between B2B and B2C marketing is the use of personal selling as a communication channel. B2B companies have been required to use personal selling in order to make sales for a number of reasons.

Often a buyer wants the reassurance of meeting someone from a supplier. Whether the purchase is costing a lot of money, of strategic importance, or both, there is risk involved. A face-to-face interaction helps reduce this risk in the mind of the customer. Having quality suppliers is often vital to the survival of many organizations. It is generally deemed important for buyers to create relationships with suppliers who will give them confidence that they can deliver over the long term.

While personal selling is a function of marketing (part of the communication piece in the marketing mix) the reality is that in most organizations it is split and treated as a separate discipline. Once a distinct sales department is being used as the primary channel to close deals, it does change the nature of marcom activities.

In many categories of consumer communications, marketing has to affect the final purchase. For example, in fast-moving consumer goods such as drinks, confectionery and toiletries, it is marcom that has to influence an individual to place Andrex toilet paper into their shopping cart. Kimberly-Clark, the owners of Andrex, do not employ salespeople in supermarkets throughout the UK to 'close' orders of toilet rolls.

However, in business-to-business marcom, often the best outcome that can be achieved is 'awareness', 'interest' or a 'lead' created.

It is unrealistic that an enterprise would invest significant amounts of money, with any provider, without meeting someone from the organization. Therefore, it will be up to the sales department to convert interest into a customer. This has meant that in the business-to-business world the singular measure of the marketing department is often the leads it generates [2]. In fact, marketing is often seen as simply existing to serve the sales team [3].

Even with personal selling, it would be more appropriate to distinguish its use by category than by using the blunt instrument of B2B and B2C. Where consumers buy big-ticket items, perceive there is a large risk in the purchase, or require an ongoing relationship with a supplier, personal selling has traditionally been used in certain B2C categories. For example, consumers have historically interacted with an estate agent when buying a house or a salesperson when purchasing a car. It is likely that before making investment decisions using a financial advisor that a consumer would want to meet them.

Furthermore, this distinction with personal selling is becoming less apparent in the digital world. All the evidence suggests that with the growing amount of information online, both consumer [4] and business purchasers are going much further down the buying journey on their own than in previous times [5]. They are using the vast sources of knowledge that can be obtained from websites, articles, blogs and videos and then utilizing peer reviews, testimonials and comments on social platforms and in forums to validate this material.

The tactics used by businesses when white papers, exclusive articles and webinars were offered in return for an email address, to enable companies to carry on promoting their offerings to prospects after they have 'opted in', are becoming less effective [6]. With an abundance of material available, savvy purchasers don't want to receive the endless promotional messages they inevitably get when providing their details. When this data is requested they simply go elsewhere.

These trends have a number of ramifications. First, the channels to market that B2C and B2B companies traditionally utilized were distinct. While B2C businesses advertised on TV, radio, in newspapers and consumer magazines, B2B companies would promote themselves in trade titles, at exhibitions and have salespeople knocking on doors and making cold calls. Of course, there was a degree of overlap. Some consumer businesses made telemarketing calls and attended lifestyle exhibitions. A few huge multinationals in the B2B space would advertise on TV and both utilized direct mail. But on the whole, there was a fair degree of separation.

Today, with the vast majority of companies utilizing social media, having websites and putting out online videos, the channels being used in both B2C and B2B marcom are more closely aligned than ever before. With the onset of digital, even TV, with its ability to personalize and target specific market segments, is much more viable for B2B brands than it was previously.

Second, B2C customers were largely anonymous to brands. They would guide themselves through purchase journeys by browsing in stores, talking to friends and reading magazines. By contrast, in the B2B world prospects would reveal themselves to possible suppliers very early on. Before the web, general information about a business offering was not widely available. Interested buyers would either have to meet a salesperson or, at the very least, request a brochure. Either activity would flag them as a potential customer who could be followed up. Today, this is not the case. Business purchasers can go through almost the entire purchase journey, having made virtually all the buying decisions, before any possible supplier is made aware. Therefore, increasingly the B2B landscape is becoming more like B2C.

In the B2C world, one of the solutions businesses utilize to attract anonymous customers is to build brand. Brand awareness is the way that consumer offerings try to ensure they are in the buying set of their customers [4]. This is now increasingly important in the B2B environment, too. While in the B2C world marcom was often brand led, in B2B the majority of organizations were sales led. Salespeople 'bashed down doors', developed relationships and closed deals. The marketing department was the support act, producing literature such as brochures, and charged with obtaining additional leads for salespeople.

With anonymous buyers taking themselves through the majority of the purchase journey, and unwilling to respond favourably to salespeople's cold approaches [6], this has now become important for B2B enterprises as well.

As we have seen throughout this myth there are an overwhelming number of similarities between business-to-business and business-to-consumer marketing. The distinctions are simply not as stark as is often assumed. The migration of buying journeys online means that not only is there less difference between B2B and B2C marketing today, they are probably more aligned and similar than ever before.

Notes

1 Cohn, C (2015) Differences in selling B2B vs B2C, *Forbes.com*, 16 June [online] www.forbes.com/sites/chuckcohn/2015/06/16/differences-in-selling-b2b-vs-b2c/#418fb83d4fb2 (archived at https://perma.cc/9Y8M-JJL7) [accessed 06 August 2018]

2 Corliss, R (2017) 15 Metrics every marketing manager should be tracking [blog] *Hubspot.com*, 28 July [online] blog.hubspot.com/blog/tabid/6307/bid/34179/15-metrics-every-marketing-manager-should-be-tracking.aspx (archived at https://perma.cc/AP77-N6GL) [accessed 07 August 2018]

3 Kotler, P, Rackham, N and Krishnaswamy, S (2006) Ending the war between sales and marketing, *Harvard Business Review*, August [online] hbr.org/2006/07/ending-the-war-between-sales-and-marketing (archived at https://perma.cc/Q6JF-WTTE) [accessed 07 August 2018]

4 Court, D et al (2009) The consumer decision journey, *McKinsey*, June [online] www.mckinsey.com/business-functions/marketing-and-sales/our-insights/the-consumer-decision-journey (archived at https://perma.cc/SRY5-JXRF) [accessed 08 August 2018]

5 Erskine, R (2017) How to turn B2B buyers into sales leads, according to data, *Forbes*, 28 December [online] www.forbes.com/sites/ryanerskine/2017/12/28/how-to-turn-b2b-buyers-into-sales-leads-according-to-data/ (archived at https://perma.cc/B652-QAP4) [accessed 08 August 2018]

6 Casey, S (2017) The birth of the B2B consumer: adopt a B2C mindset to meet buyers' changing preferences. *Forrester*, 5 October [online] d3oxih60gx1ls6.cloudfront.net/fde7e5e8-204e-4647-9bec-7ad5c41d42b6/980e74e0-3038-4ec7-8205-b2957885873b_The_Birth_Of_The_B2B_Consumer.pdf (archived at https://perma.cc/LM59-DF7T) [accessed 08 August 2018]

MYTH
13

EFFECTIVE MARCOM MEANS RUNNING A SERIES OF GREAT CAMPAIGNS

Before the World Wide Web, marcom activity was often based around a series of campaigns [1]. When companies had to pay each time they wanted to reach their prospects, it was beyond the budgets of most organizations to be in front of their target audience on an ongoing basis.

In order to obtain the most from their spend, it made sense for communications to be coordinated around particular themes, or offerings, and utilized at pertinent times of the year. So, holiday companies sent out brochures in January and February when a large percentage of the population were thinking about their summer holiday. Gyms ran promotions to join in the new year when people made resolutions to get fit, and stationery suppliers had seasonal offers to entice people to their stores just before children went back to school for the new academic year.

For example, a department store may have chosen to co-ordinate some television commercials, print media advertising and direct mail all based around its Christmas offering. In this case, the campaign, running for six weeks before the holidays, was specifically designed to drive footfall onto its website, and in-store, in order to increase its share of the Christmas market. We can extrapolate from this scenario that a marketing campaign is 'a coordinated series of activities, with a particular theme and/or focus, designed to fulfil a defined goal or goals over a specific period of time' [2].

Businesses still utilize campaigns for a number of different reasons. There are particular times of year where it may make sense for an organization to put additional resources into its communications as the offering it has is more likely to be on its audience's agenda. An enterprise may also deem it worthwhile to invest in campaigns around other occurrences, such as the launching of a new product or service, a sales drive, a concerted effort to increase brand awareness or participation in a particular event or exhibition.

Sometimes a one-off opportunity may present itself and a business decides to take advantage. For example, when Alan Pardew, the then manager of Newcastle United Football Club, head-butted Hull midfielder David Meyler on the side of the pitch [3], the betting company Paddy Power decided to piggyback off the publicity the story was receiving. It ran a promotion offering a 'money back special' should Newcastle score a headed goal in their next game against Fulham [4].

As we can see from these examples, there are many occasions when companies will run promotional campaigns. But these can no longer be the sole focus of an organization's communications activities as they once were. Today, with 88 per cent of consumers [5] and 94 per cent of B2B purchasers conducting some form of web research before buying [6], having a significant and 'always on' presence online, as opposed to merely running seasonal or ad-hoc campaigns, is a necessity for virtually all businesses.

Media such as websites, blogs, Facebook pages, YouTube channels and Instagram accounts are comparable to any other media; like TV and radio, they are only as good as the content that is put on them. No one would keep watching a TV channel that constantly showed the same programme, nor would they listen to a radio station that only had one show. Similarly, these online platforms need to be constantly updated with fresh content to keep them vibrant, interesting and engaging.

With this being the case, enterprises can no longer silo their communications activities to a few particular moments and campaigns throughout the year.

If a prospect visits a website or Facebook page, for example, and it is clear that it has not been updated in a while, they are likely to simply look elsewhere [7]. Regular content is vital in encouraging ongoing engagement with prospects and customers. By staying front of mind, companies can ensure they are in the buying set of potential customers when they are ready to make a purchase. Regular content is also key in search engine optimization (SEO) [8]. Search engines demand fresh material for a business to rank highly in any search results.

Understanding this, it's clear that promotions can no longer be an activity designated to certain times of the year. This is now an ongoing discipline with which companies need to perennially engage.

In some ways it can be helpful to distinguish an activity by categorizing it as having an 'earned audience' or a 'paid for' audience. 'Earned audience' is made up of the prospects and customers who discover a business through the worthwhile material they create and post online. It is also the audience whose attention is retained and nurtured by providing valuable content.

The 'paid for' audience gains awareness of the brand through activities such as promotions run on platforms like LinkedIn and Facebook, commercials created for TV and radio, and offers sent out via direct mail. To be sure, the content used in advertising can still be value led. The difference is that a business is paying to ensure it gets in front of the right eyeballs. Having 'paid for' the initial exchange, a business may need to nurture the recognition it has won. The ongoing interaction with the prospect is 'earned' from that time.

For example, commercials during the Super Bowl are the most expensive advertising slots in the world. The cost of a 30-second ad, in 2018, was US $5 million [9]. Understandably, companies want to obtain the most awareness they can for their investment. The millions of dollars that an organization spends for a 30-second slot 'pays for' attention. In order to get bang for its buck, a corporation wants to leverage this attention to drive further engagement, much of which will be 'earned'. The internet makes this possible.

For example, in 2018, over 20 companies released their TV adverts online before the Super Bowl took place [10]. The top three commercials had amassed almost 30 million views between them, with Budweiser's 'Stand by You' and Amazon's 'Alexa Loses Her Voice' advertisements receiving over 10 million views each [11].

Just a few months after Super Bowl 52, the top commercials such as Groupon's 'Who Wouldn't' [12], Budweiser's 'Stand By You' [13] and Bud Light's 'The Bud Knight' [14] had all amassed around 20 million views on YouTube alone, while Amazon's 'Alexa Loses Her Voice' had 45 million views on the platform [15]. Advertisers also created hashtags in order to drive engagement. For instance, the brand Avocados from Mexico had 83,132 mentions on Twitter with its hashtag #Guacworld [16].

It should be noted that virtually all the commercials that did well during the Super Bowl were either really humorous, or very sentimental and resonated with people emotionally. Consequently, as well as promoting the brand they also provided 'value' by being entertaining. If they had been purely promotional messages, with no inherent value on offer, it is extremely unlikely these companies would have garnered as much engagement online, despite purchasing one of the most expensive TV advertising slots in the world.

This kind of blended approach can be very effective. With so much noise in the marketplace, cutting through organically is not easy. Whether it is running commercials on TV or radio, placing print advertising in magazines and newspapers, sending out direct mail or spending money to promote content on platforms such as Facebook, LinkedIn or Twitter, there will be a commercial case to 'pay for' awareness at given times. Campaigns, therefore, still have a useful part to play in the marcom strategy of many companies.

Attention is now one of the most precious resources on earth [17]. Inhabiting a world with an abundance of information has led to attention becoming scarce. If some recognition can be 'earned' by utilizing SEO, distributing content through the appropriate media channels and as a result of social sharing, these activities will be an important part of the marcom mix. Once a company has obtained the awareness of a prospect or customer, using its media channels to create regular engagement can keep them front of mind and negate the need to keep 'paying for' their attention over and over again.

Communications used to be an event for lots of businesses, with many enterprises merely running a few specific campaigns at certain times of the year. While these campaigns may still play a part, the importance of digital channels, and their demand for constant endeavour, means that marcom now has to be an ongoing element of day-to-day operations. It can no longer be seen as a rare occurrence. Marcom, therefore, is no longer a series of great campaigns but a continuous activity that may require specifically focused campaigns, at strategic points in the year, as part of the communications that are undertaken.

Notes

1 ORACLE/Responsys (2013) Making the Shift: How great marketers are changing their focus from the campaign to the customer [online] www.oracle.com/partners/en/products/cloud-solutions/oracle-marketing-cloud-hub/customer-centric-marketing-2539859.pdf (archived at https://perma.cc/ZV2F-6HD3) [accessed 01 August 2018]

2 Big Commerce (nd) What are marketing campaigns? [online] www.bigcommerce.co.uk/ecommerce-answers/what-are-marketing-campaigns/ (archived at https://perma.cc/84UE-FD2G) [accessed 02 October 2018]

3 Taylor, L (2014) Alan Pardew handed seven-game ban for head-butting Hull's David Meyler, *Guardian*, 11 March [online] www.theguardian.com/football/2014/mar/11/alan-pardew-seven-games-ban-head-butt (archived at https://perma.cc/48YV-FFK5) [accessed 08 August 2018]

4 Jackson, L A (2014) Alan Pardew headbutt inspires Paddy Power for new money back special – refunds if Magpies scores a headed goal in next league match, *Online Betting*, 05 March [online] www.online-betting.me.uk/news/alan-pardew-headbutt-inspires-paddy-power-for-new-money-back-special.html (archived at https://perma.cc/9B7A-6K65) [accessed 08 August 2018]

5 Stewart, T (2018) US consumers like to research products online before buying in-store, *Mobile Marketing Magazine*, 10 January [online] mobilemarketingmagazine.com/us-consumers-ecommerce-2017 (archived at https://perma.cc/ZPN5-HR4U) [accessed 08 August 2018]

6 Accenture Interactive (2014) Point of View Series – 2014 state of B2B procurement study: online product research and price comparison popular among B2B buyers [online] www.accenture.com/t20150624T211502__w__/us-en/_acnmedia/Accenture/Conversion-Assets/DotCom/Documents/Global/PDF/Industries_15/Accenture-B2B-Procurement-Study.pdf (archived at https://perma.cc/F2VF-6RBD) [accessed 08 August 2018]

7 Lake, C (2010) 25 reasons why I'll leave your website in 10 seconds [blog] *Econsultancy.com*, 1 December [online] econsultancy.com/blog/6924-25-reasons-why-i-ll-leave-your-website-in-10-seconds (archived at https://perma.cc/2MCU-2Z4A) [accessed 08 August 2018]

8 Patel, N (nd) Why SEO is actually all about content marketing [blog] [online] neilpatel.com/blog/seo-is-content-marketing/ (archived at https://perma.cc/Z5P6-QQY2) [accessed 08 August 2018]

9 Michaels, M (2018) The price of a 30-second Super Bowl ad has exploded – but it may be worth it for companies, *businessinsider.com*, 25 January [online] https://www.businessinsider.com/super-bowl-commercials-cost-more-than-eagles-quarterback-earns-2018-1?r=US&IR=T (archived at https://perma.cc/LPN9-DQZS) [accessed 17 March 2019]

10 Rodriguez, A (2018) This year's Super Bowl commercials may actually surprise you, *Quartz*, 01 February [online] qz.com/1194407/this-years-super-bowl-commercials-may-actually-surprise-you/ (archived at https://perma.cc/46GA-DFXK) [accessed 08 August 2018]

11 Alexander, R (2018) Brands are leaking Super Bowl ads early. This is the No. 1 most viral ad so far, *Moneyish.com*, 03 March [online] moneyish.com/ish/brands-are-leaking-super-bowl-ads-early-this-is-the-no-1-most-viral-ad-so-far/ (archived at https://perma.cc/5MU9-LR26) [accessed 08 August 2018]

12 Groupon (2018) Groupon 2018 Super Bowl Commercial, 'Who Wouldn't' [online] https://www.youtube.com/watch?v=GM1QDBvzm1Y (archived at https://perma.cc/FM5A-JN6H) [accessed 08 August 2018] *'Published on Jan 25, 2018. 21,362,855 views'*

13 Budweiser (2018) Budweiser Super Bowl Commercial 2018, 'Stand By You' [online] www.youtube.com/watch?v=GNVw5f16GEM (archived at https://perma.cc/HA7G-4VYR) [accessed 02 October 2018]. NB: Original Budweiser 10.3m+ YouTube views version www.youtube.com/watch?v=CxGUmtRLm5g (archived at https://perma.cc/6RB2-FH7R) not available online at time of going to press

14 Bud Light (2018) Bud Light – The Bud Knight [online] www.youtube.com (archived at https://perma.cc/XL5E-NZWH) [accessed 08 August 2018]

15 Amazon (2018) Alexa Loses Her Voice – Amazon Super Bowl LII Commercial (Online video) Available from: www.youtube.com (archived at https://perma.cc/XL5E-NZWH) [accessed 08 August 2018]

16 Swant, M (2018) Avocados from Mexico, Pepsi and Doritos Won the first half of the Super Bowl on Twitter, *AdWeek*, 04 February [online] www.adweek.com/digital/avocados-from-mexico-pepsi-and-doritos-won-the-first-half-of-super-bowl-on-twitter/ (archived at https://perma.cc/78W3-8E2Q) [accessed 08 August 2018]

17 MacGregor, P (2016) Why attention is the world's most valuable resource, *Marketing Magazine*, 29 July [online] www.marketingmag.com.au/hubs-c/attention-worlds-valuable-resource/ (archived at https://perma.cc/R9BT-HVSS) [accessed 08 August 2018]

A SUCCESSFUL BUSINESS REQUIRES A COMPELLING USP

The USP (Unique Selling Proposition) was created by Rosser Reeves, who worked for an advertising agency called Ted Bates & Co. Having developed the idea of the USP throughout the 1950s, Reeves explained the concept in his 1961 book, *Reality in Advertising* [1]. In it he explained the USP has three parts:

1 'Each advertisement must say to each reader: buy this product, and you will get this specific benefit.'

2 'It must be unique – either a uniqueness of the brand or a claim not otherwise made in that particular field of advertising.'

3 'The proposition must be so strong that it can move the mass millions, ie pull over new customers to your product.'

Perhaps one of the most famous examples of a USP that Rosser Reeves created was the slogan, 'It melts in your mouth, not in your hands', developed for M&Ms, which at the time were the first chocolates in the US market to be coated in a hard shell [2].

The USP has moved from being an approach developed for the world of advertising to becoming a concept broadly used throughout the world of marketing. While it is hard to understand exactly why this transition occurred, it may be because the USP is synonymous with the idea of 'differentiation', which is widely considered vital for a business to be successful.

The importance of 'product differentiation' was first proposed by the economist Edward Chamberlin, who coined the phrase in his 1933 doctoral thesis, 'Theory for Monopolistic Competition' [3]. In more recent times, individuals such as Harvard Marketing Professor Theodore Levitt, who wrote a seminal article, 'Marketing Success Through Differentiation – of Anything' [4] and Michael Porter, whose book *Competitive Strategy* is widely regarded as a classic work in the approach to modern business [5], have both emphasized the importance of differentiation.

One could question the validity of the USP, even during the 1950s when the concept was first developed. By definition, the USP is all about 'what' a company does – 'buy this product and obtain these benefits'. It is hard to imagine how more than one or two companies, in any product category, could have an offering that was genuinely unique. Yet there are many categories that contain more than one or two successful products. For example, the category of toilet paper contains a number of successful businesses. There were three brands of toilet paper in the United States in 2018 that were used by over 50 million consumers: Charmin Ultra, Scott Tissue and Angel Soft. Meanwhile, 75 million consumers used a store brand [6]. Despite their popularity, these different brands of toilet paper did not each have unique benefits unrivalled by the others. Be that as it may, in a world of far less choice than there is today, when people were generally tied to sourcing products and services within their locality [7], the USP may have had some efficacy.

But now, in the global economic environment in which businesses operate, the idea of a USP is delusive.

Any enterprise that provides intangible services, for example, financial advisers, training companies, law firms etc, is unable to promise anything that cannot immediately be copied by a competitor.

Of course, it does not mean that any of these organizations cannot innovate and come up with a new idea. But by definition the promise is intangible. The likelihood is that other firms will be able to make the same offering to their clients and prospects, if they choose to do so.

While it is almost inconceivable to have a USP in services, it is more feasible that the originators of products could potentially have something unique. In theory, a tangible item that needs to be manufactured will take more time to copy. Also, while it is impossible to own an idea, it is easier to legally protect discernible products with physical features and processes by way of patents [8]. Although this is the case, the speed at which the global economy moves means companies do not have their USP for very long.

For example, the Apple iPad was groundbreaking. Although one of the first tablet computers available in the market was GRiD Systems' GRiDPad in 1988, and many companies had attempted to launch tablets thereafter [9], it was the iPad with its touchscreen interface that transformed the market. It was the first tablet to be widely adopted, selling 19 million units in its first year [10]. In fact, it was so successful it changed the technology landscape, resulting in fewer sales of laptop computers [11].

The Apple iPad first went on sale at the beginning of April 2010 [12]. Yet, despite being a proprietary piece of technology, Apple's first mover advantage was short-lived. The Dell 'Streak' went on sale in August 2010 [13], while the Samsung 'Galaxy Tab' was available in November of the same year [14]. By the Spring of 2011 there were a multitude of options by companies such as Motorola, Asus and HP amongst others [15]. In other words, if Apple did have a USP, it was short lived.

Of course, if a company can truly disrupt a market, introducing a new product or service with a genuinely compelling innovation, then this is likely to bring with it commercial success, even if its unique proposition doesn't last long. These businesses, though, are the few exceptions, not the rule. There are plenty of flourishing organizations that have never been unique. How many success-ful law firms, recruitment agents and management consultancies can claim to have started with a market-changing unique selling proposition?

The reality is that enterprises do not need a USP in order to be successful. For many companies it is not 'what' they do that makes them attractive but 'how' they do it and for 'whom'. For example, Apple is a premium brand. Its products are more expensive than many of its competitors. It therefore targets higher earners and demographic groups that will be able to afford its products [16].

Like with any premium brand, the higher price imbues Apple products with a feeling of status and exclusivity that cheaper and more accessible products cannot provide. It has higher profit margins than its competitors selling similar products [17]. This enables it to invest in elegant packaging and great retail experiences, which reinforces its market position. Despite its undeniable success, the iPhone has tended to have around 15–20 per cent of global market share for a number of years [18], clearly showing that while it is hugely popular, it is not for everybody.

Similarly, an accountancy firm is unlikely to differentiate itself by what it does. Core services such as management accounts, finan-cial planning, audits and tax advice will be offered by almost every accountancy practice. However, an accountancy firm may decide to specialize in working with fast-growth entrepreneurial businesses within a 50-mile radius of its premises. This being the case, it may cultivate relationships with angel investors, start a networking group for its entrepreneur clients to meet monthly at its premises in order to share knowledge, experiences and best practice, and specialize in providing advice to enable businesses to scale up effectively. This accountancy firm will have no USP, as what is does is no different from any other accountants. There will not be any one single aspect of its offering that it could state is unique. It will be the whole pack-age of 'how' it delivers its service, shaped by 'who' it delivers it for, that will make it particularly attractive to a specific market.

Targeting a specific 'who' and creating a 'how' that is compelling for that particular audience will enable any business to become more appealing than it would otherwise be with a more generic offering. While this is not a USP, it will allow an organization to differentiate itself to a point. Of course, there could be another competitor that decides to target the same audience. So, while this approach might decrease the number of direct competitors, it doesn't necessarily provide a firm with an unconstrained competitive advantage.

It's clear from these examples that the USP and differentiation are not necessarily the same thing, but despite this they have largely become synonymous with each other. It has become common parlance that in order to be successful, a company has to be different. This very often leads to talk about coming up with a USP. But as Byron Sharp demonstrated in his book *How Brands Grow* [19], this is simply not the case.

Coca-Cola and Pepsi are two of the most famous, successful and iconic brands of all time [20]. Yet neither have a USP. In fact, they are not even different. Technically, the drinks don't taste the same and one cannot dispute that given a direct choice between the two, people may have a preference. Despite this, for a large majority of consumers, if they ask for a Coke in a bar and the person serving states they only stock Pepsi, most individuals will opt for the Pepsi [21] rather than choose a completely different drink. This demonstrates that the difference in taste is not meaningful for most customers.

Trainers from Adidas and Nike are a similar example. While individuals may have a preference for one brand over the other, neither has a USP or is tangibly different. Yet, these are two of the most successful sportswear brands in the world. McDonald's and Burger King demonstrate this continuing pattern. While many consumers may have a predilection for one over the other, and they don't technically taste the same, for most consumers they are interchangeable. If one were to desire fast food, and only one of these brands was available, the vast majority would be happy to settle for whichever was accessible at the time [22].

While this is true for these well-known consumer brands it is no less applicable to the business world. For example, the Big Four accountancy and consulting firms Ernst & Young, Deloitte, KPMG and PricewaterhouseCoopers have no USPs or meaningful differentiators. Yet, between them they are responsible for auditing 80 per cent of all US public companies [23].

Of course, if a company *can* create a compelling USP, or be truly different in a way that is meaningful for customers, it will assist it in its commercial endeavours. What these examples show is that one does not *need* a USP or meaningful differentiators to be successful.

Above all, a business must be distinctive. What all these organizations – from Coca-Cola to Nike, McDonald's to Adidas and KPMG to PricewaterhouseCoopers – have in common is that they are distinctive. That is, they are considered excellent in their sector, mean something to the market and can be distinguished by their names, logo and other brand assets.

It's true these companies are global leaders known and recognized throughout the world, but a company does not have to be recognized by the entire planet to be distinctive. Even if a company does not have a USP or differentiator, whichever marketplace or 'who' it chooses to service should recognize the name, be able to distinguish it visually and understand that it stands for excellence within its chosen field. As these big brands demonstrate, distinctiveness in a target market can be enough to have a successful business.

Notes

1 Reeves, R (1961) *Reality in Advertising*, Knopf, Inc., New York
2 Schultz, E J (2013) Rewind: 1954 ad shows M&MS characters go for a chocolatey swim, Black & White Spot for the Mars brand helped propel now-famous tagline, *AdAge*, 09 May [online]

adage.com/article/rewind/1954- ad-shows-m-ms-characters-a-chocolatey-swim/241375/ (archived at https://perma.cc/9V6W-2HQ2) [09 August 2018]

3 Encyclopaedia Britannica, Editors (2018) Edward Hastings Chamberlin – American economist. Encyclopaedia Britannica, 12 July [online] www.britannica.com/biography/Edward-Hastings-Chamberlin#ref44945 (archived at https://perma.cc/WV5P-BKZH) [accessed 09 August 2018]

4 Levitt, T (1980) Marketing success through differentiation – of anything, *Harvard Business Review*, January [online] hbr.org/1980/01/marketing-success-through-differentiation-of-anything (archived at https://perma.cc/K6AX-BNP4 [accessed 09 August 2018]

5 Porter, M (1980*) Competitive Strategy: Techniques for analyzing industries and competitors*, The Free Press, New York

6 Statista (2018) US population: Which brands of toilet paper do you use most often? Numbers of consumers (in millions) [online] https://www.statista.com/statistics/275967/us-households-most-used-brands-of-toilet-paper/ (archived at https://perma.cc/X9CV-G8HS) [accessed 17 March 2019]

7 KPMG (2017) The truth about online consumers: 2017 Global Online Consumer Report [online] assets.kpmg.com/content/dam/kpmg/xx/pdf/2017/01/the-truth-about-online-consumers.pdf (archived at https://perma.cc/6BJX-FSLD) [accessed 06 October 2018]

8 GOV.UK (nd) Patenting your invention [online] www.gov.uk/patent-your-invention (archived at https://perma.cc/S3XQ-N25F) [accessed 09 August 2018]

9 Steele, C (2011) History of the tablet. From our caveman days to the present, how the tablet – and we – have evolved, *PC Mag*, 07 August [online] www.pcmag.com/feature/285757/history-of-the-tablet (archived at https://perma.cc/R4UL-SQTH) [accessed 09 August 2018]

10 Vogelstein, F(2013) How Steve Jobs made the iPad succeed when all other tablets failed, *Wired*, 11 February [online] www.wired.com/2013/11/one-ipad-to-rule-them-all-all-those-who-dream-big-are-not-lost/ (archived at https://perma.cc/9BZA-VLZT) [accessed 09 August 2018]

11 Goldman, D (2011) iPad cuts 'dramatically' into laptop PC sales, *CNNMoney*, 03 March [online] money.cnn.com/2011/03/03/technology/tablet_pc/index.htm (archived at https://perma.cc/2AU6-D2AM) [accessed 09 August 2018]

12 Kastrenakes, J (2015) The iPad's 5th anniversary: a timeline of Apple's category-defining tablet, *The Verge*, 03 April [online] www.theverge.com/2015/4/3/8339599/apple-ipad-five-years-old-timeline-photos-videos (archived at https://perma.cc/B3CC-HZL2) [accessed 09 August 2018]

13 Wilhelm, A (2010) Dell streak on sale in the US August 12th, *The Next Web*, 10 August [online] thenextweb.com/mobile/2010/08/10/dell-streak-on-sale-in-the-us-august-12th/ (archived at https://perma.cc/JH75-7944) [accessed 09 August 2018]

14 Chacksfield, M (2010) Samsung Galaxy Tab UK launch date: 1 November, *Techradar*, 1 October [online] https://www.techradar.com/uk/news/mobile-computing/tablets/samsung-galaxy-tab-uk-release-date-1-november-720485 (archived at https://perma.cc/2DFD-JEDJ) [accessed 09 August 2018]

15 Hiner, J (2011) Top 10 tablets of 2011, the new leaderboard, *ZDNet*, 04 April [online] www.zdnet.com/article/top-10-tablets-of-2011-the-new-leaderboard/ (archived at https://perma.cc/4U87-MRGP) [accessed 09 August 2018]

16 Dudovsskiy, J (2018) Apple segmentation, targeting and positioning, *Research-Methodology*, 18 January [online] research-methodology.net/apple-segmentation-targeting-and-positioning/ (archived at https://perma.cc/F3T5-HJXC) [accessed 09 August 2018]

17 Dunn, J (2017) Samsung introduced 10 times as many phones as Apple last year, but its mobile division made half as much revenue, *UK Business Insider*, 27 February [online] uk.businessinsider.com/samsung-vs-apple-galaxy-iphone-smartphone-revenue-chart-2017-2?r=US&IR=T (archived at https://perma.cc/69SZ-B28T) [accessed 09 August 2018]

18 Statista (2018) Global smartphone shipments market share by vendor from the 2nd quarter 2014 to the 2nd quarter 2018 [online] www.statista.com/statistics/671213/worldwide-market-share-of-leading-smartphone-manufacturers/ (archived at https://perma.cc/F3JJ-NK22) [accessed 09 August 2019]

19 Sharp, B (2010) *How Brands Grow: What marketers don't know*, Oxford University Press, Melbourne

20 Cohn, M and Bromell, M (2013) The 50 most iconic brand logos of all time, *Complex*, 07 March [online] www.complex.com/life/2013/03/the-50-most-iconic-brand-logos-of-all-time/ (archived at https://perma.cc/YNU4-JHF3) [accessed 09 August 2018]

21 Potter, J (2017) Is it ok if I just serve a Pepsi to my customers who ask for Coke? *Quora*, 31 October [online] www.quora.com/Is-it-ok-if-I-just-serve-a-Pepsi-to-my-customers-who-ask-for-Coke (archived at https://perma.cc/E9BK-2AZG) [accessed 09 August 2018]

22 These two contradictory quotes from the same page on Quora.com illustrate my point... (1) Dai Adrian (2016) Should I eat McDonalds or Burger King? *Quora.com*, 20 March [online] www.quora.com/Should-I-eat-McDonalds-or-Burger-King (archived at https://perma.cc/7FK4-JMSN) [accessed 05 October 2018]; (2) Pagare, R (2016) Should I eat McDonalds or Burger King? *Quora.com*, 22 February [online] www.quora.com/Should-I-eat-McDonalds-or-Burger-King (archived at https://perma.cc/7FK4-JMSN) [accessed 05 October 2018]

23 The Big 4 Accounting Firms [online] big4accountingfirms.org/ (archived at https://perma.cc/DQK9-VA4U) [accessed 09 August 2018]

MARKET POSITIONING IS ALL ABOUT THE PRODUCT OR SERVICE ON OFFER

In 1968, Coca-Cola and Pepsi dominated the soft drinks market in the United States. Almost two-thirds of all sales of carbonated soft drinks were colas [1]. In other words, when someone wanted a soft drink, cola was the first choice. Within this context, trying to persuade American consumers that they shouldn't drink cola but should change to 7 Up instead should have been futile.

But the creative team in the Chicago office of the agency J. Walter Thompson pulled a masterstroke in market positioning. In 1968, adverts were released referring to 7 Up as the 'uncola' [2]. In other words, rather than try to steal market share from Coca-Cola and Pepsi, 7 Up was positioned as 'the' alternative choice. So, on those occasions when someone didn't fancy a cola they automatically thought of 7 Up. The campaign leveraged what was already in the customer's mind, that 'cola is the natural choice for a soft drink', and made 7 Up the obvious alternative. In the first year of the campaign sales of 7 Up doubled [3].

In 1997, Steve Jobs returned to Apple as Interim CEO, having left in 1985 [4]. Apple was on the verge of bankruptcy and needed an investment from Microsoft to stay afloat. Microsoft came to Apple's rescue with a $150 million investment. [5]. At that time, Steve Jobs hired TBWA/Chiat/Day to undertake an advertising campaign. It was this agency that came up with the slogan 'Think Different'.

Craig Tanimoto, who wrote the phrase [6], was reacting to 'Think IBM', a campaign that was running for IBM's Thinkpad [7], although 'Think' had first been used as an expression by IBM as early as 1915 [8]. IBM was then the second-biggest maker of personal computers [9]. As one of the oldest computer companies in the world [10], it was very much an 'establishment' brand. The 'Think Different' idiom leveraged existing perceptions in the marketplace, and positioned Apple as distinct and unlike other companies within its sector. Despite launching no new products at the time, Apple still received a boost from the campaign and within 12 months its stock price had tripled. It paved the way for its successful launch of multicoloured iMacs a year later [6].

These examples highlight two major rules of market positioning. First, market positioning is not always about the product. Referring to 7 Up as the 'uncola' is not really about the drink – after all, it could have been a carbonated orange or apple beverage. Rather, this positioning worked solely in relation to customer perceptions of the market. It gave 7 Up a place in the mind of the customer.

Second, customer perceptions are all that matter. For example, the first cars were referred to as 'horseless carriages' [11]. Describing something as an automobile would not have appealed to the understanding of the time, when many everyday folk would simply not have appreciated what it was.

Human beings don't believe what we see; we see what we believe [12]. In other words, our preconceived conceptions will influence how we process information and make evaluations. This reality is extremely important in marketing communications.

For all the attention that an organization manages to obtain from its target market, in the totality of an individual's existence, it will be a miniscule amount of time. In these limited moments, a business has to communicate ideas that will resonate. It is almost impossible for an individual to process information that doesn't fit with their paradigm of how the world works. Messages that contradict their current frame of reference are most likely to be ignored.

So it follows that in order for a company's marcom to be really effective, it needs to understand the perceptions that its audience already holds. It can then leverage this understanding as the basis for any communication. Market positioning happens in the mind of the customer. This is ultimately what defines market positioning, which is influencing perception in order to occupy a clear and desirable position in the mind of the customer.

For example, Volvo's market positioning is synonymous with safety [13]. Of course, on a practical level other leading brands such as BMW, Honda and Ford are also safe cars. In fact, all manufacturers in Europe have to adhere to the same set of safety standards [14]. Yet, in the mind of the customer it is Volvo which is the 'safe' vehicle. Having introduced the concept of three-point safety belts in 1959, a standard still used today [15], Volvo could communicate its credentials to consumers and own this position in the market. It has reinforced this with other innovations over the years.

Volvo's ownership of the word safety highlights other rules of market positioning. 'Safety' is easily intelligible, and in the context of cars, an important consideration. In a world where grabbing attention is a challenge, to cut through and be able to occupy a place in the customer's mind, the message must be elegantly simple.

The message must also be consistent. Occupying a desirable place inside a customer's mind is an achievement many companies never accomplish. Unless a successful position becomes commercially irrelevant, to let it go voluntarily is often short-sighted. Individuals who live with a position, and message, everyday within a business, can become fatigued and start believing that it needs refreshing. Conversely, customers who only give these communications momentary thought on an irregular basis are unlikely to be bored. Changing a position can easily leave customers confused and less likely to consider the offering when making a purchase.

Being first to occupy a market position is decisive [16], and once a brand does own a position in the market, it is extremely difficult to dislodge them. 'Confirmation bias' is the tendency for human beings to process information in a way that is consistent with their current beliefs [17]. Once a consumer has placed Volvo as the 'safe' car in their mind, it is almost impossible for another manufacturer to convince them that it is safer.

Finding a compelling position is pivotal in creating successful marcom. As David Ogilvy, one of the legends of advertising, articulated, positioning means deciding 'what the product does and who it is for' [18]. In 1972, Ogilvy ran an advert entitled 'How to create advertising that sells' [19]. In the advert he stated that the most important decision to be made was 'How do you position your product?' He asks, 'Should you position SCHWEPPES as a soft drink – or as a mixer? Should you position DOVE as a product for dry skin or as a product which gets hands really clean?' [20]

In fact, Ogilvy's positioning of Dove soap was a roaring success [21]. Having previously worked at George Gallup's Audience Research Institute [22], Ogilvy was fastidious with his analysis of any product and market. Having asked to see the formula and discovering that it was 'one quarter cleansing cream', he launched Dove as a bar for women that was good for your skin and 'makes soap old-fashioned' [23].

Similarly, in his book, *Ogilvy on Advertising*, David Ogilvy explains that SAAB had no measurable profile in Norway. He decided to position SAAB as 'the car for winter'. Of course, there were other cars in the market that would have been equally reliable in the winter time but being the first to communicate this position, SAAB became the winter car in the customer's mind. Merely three years later, SAAB was voted the best car for Norwegian winters [18].

Once a brand has a successful position in the customer's mind, it must be careful not to lose its competitive advantage by diluting the proposition. A business has to think extremely carefully about whether it should extend the product line under one brand name or introduce a completely new brand. This will depend on whether the single position will stretch convincingly into another category.

It is almost impossible for a brand to own more than one position in the customer's mind. It is not up to the business to decide whether a position will stretch to another category or not; it is all about how the customer perceives the market.

So, the Disney brand itself offers theme parks, hotels, cruises, merchandise, stores, television programmes, films, music and theatre, etc. At its core, Disney is a family entertainment and media business [24]. It could be argued that it is providing the same entertainment and content across a number of different platforms and channels. Its core emotional proposition to 'create happiness and deliver magical moments' [25] is delivered across all these experiences. In other words, its market position is consistent even though it provides a number of distinct offerings. Ultimately, it works because intuitively customers perceive it the same way.

Conversely, in 2015 Google created a new holding company, Alphabet [26], under which companies such as Boston Dynamics, which does robotics, DeepMind, working in artificial intelligence, and Nest Labs, creating solutions for the automated home and Internet of Things [27], can all exist.

Google has a market position of being number one in search [28]. To try to undertake so many different projects under the umbrella of one brand could have the effect of diminishing Google's market position and leaving customers confused. Separating these projects with their own distinct labels gives the opportunity for each one to own a place in the customer's mind within its specialist area, while not diminishing Google's brand in the eyes of the customer.

Brands with distinct positions in the customer's mind will find it extremely difficult to be considered a leader in another category, if consumers perceive the category offering as different. So, today, many major car manufacturers have some sort of electric car offering [29]. Nevertheless, if you asked most consumers the first electric vehicle brand that comes to mind, they are most likely to say 'Tesla'.

This is because Tesla's market position is as a specialist in electric cars [30], whereas companies such as General Motors, Ford and Volkswagen have a plethora of different vehicles. Just as Toyota created Lexus when it wanted to get into the luxury car market [31], it may have been a better positioning strategy for some of these companies to create a separate electric car brand.

Of course, there is a long way to go, and many other factors besides positioning will affect which companies are successful in the electric vehicle space. It is interesting to note that although it was only formed in 2003 [30], in 2017 Tesla briefly eclipsed BMW in market capitalization and was the most valuable auto manufacturer in the world [32]. With the scope, size and history of its many competitors, this is a tremendous feat and demonstrates the power of market positioning, whatever may happen to Tesla in the future.

Market positioning is one of the most important aspects of a company's marketing strategy, and can make or break the success it has. While all businesses should strive to create excellent products and services that customers will desire, positioning itself has more to do with customer perception than it does with products and services.

Of course, there has to be an authenticity to the position that is chosen. 7 Up really isn't a cola drink, Volvo has innovated in the area of car safety and Dove was really better for the skin than traditional soap. While obvious after the fact, none of these products had to be positioned in the way that we have come to know; at the time, there were other options available. Ultimately, positioning is about understanding the target market, its preconceptions, and leveraging these to occupy a desirable place in the customer's mind. Thus, when it comes to market positioning, customer perception is everything.

Notes

1 Federal Trade Commission (1999) Bureau of Economics Staff Report – Transformation and continuity: the U.S. carbonated soft drink bottling industry and antitrust policy since 1980 [online] msu.edu/~conlinmi/teaching/MBA814/softdrink.pdf (archived at https://perma.cc/7E3D-TB7R) [accessed 10 October 2018]

2 McDonald, A (2017) Uncola: Seven-Up, counterculture and the making of an American brand, *Duke University Libraries*, 04 December [online] blogs.library.duke.edu/rubenstein/2017/12/04/uncola/ (archived at https://perma.cc/6Y9Z-AJZV) [accessed 10 October 2018]

3 Editorial (2003) Seven-Up Co (7 UP, Dr Pepper/Seven Up), *AdAge*, 15 September [online] https://adage.com/article/adage-encyclopedia/7up-dr-pepper/98877 (archived at https://perma.cc/G277-93RC) [accessed 10 October 2018]

4 Dormehl, L (2018) Today in Apple history: Steve Jobs leaves and rejoins Apple, *Cult of Mac*, 16 September [online] www.cultofmac.com/445723/today-in-apple-history-steve-jobs-leaves-and-rejoins-apple/ (archived at https://perma.cc/YGY2-W3B6) [accessed 10 October 2018]

5 Shontell, A (2010) The greatest comeback story of all time: how Apple went from near bankruptcy to billions in 13 years, *Business Insider*, 26 October [online] www.businessinsider.com/apple-comeback-story-2010-10?IR=T (archived at https://perma.cc/6S5A-QXPY) [accessed 10 October 2018]

6 Siltanen, R (2011) The real story behind Apple's 'Think Different' Campaign, *Forbes*, 14 December [online] www.forbes.com/sites/onmarketing/2011/12/14/the-real-story-behind-apples-think-different-campaign/#8b802cb62abc (archived at https://perma.cc/P3JW-XHUL) [accessed 17 October 2018]

7 Greenfield, R (2011) The true history of Apple's 'Think Different' campaign, *The Atlantic*, 14 October [online] www.theatlantic.com/technology/archive/2011/12/true-history-apples-think-different-campaign/334256/ (archived at https://perma.cc/CDB8-BCWB) [accessed 10 October 2018]

8 Madrigal, Alexis C (2011) IBM's First 100 Years: A Heavily
    Illustrated Timeline. The Atlantic. 16/06. [online] www.
    theatlantic.com/technology/archive/2011/06/ibms-first-100-years-
    a-heavily-illustrated-timeline/240502/ (archived at https://perma.
    cc/28TL-QTRX) [accessed 10 October 2018]

9 Markoff, J (1997) PC industry worldwide grew by 18% last
    year, *New York Times*, 27 January [online] www.nytimes.
    com/1997/01/27/business/pc-industry-worldwide-grew-by-18-last-
    year.html (archived at https://perma.cc/2EW7-VRHA) [accessed 10
    October 2018]

10 Johnston, R (2014) 5 of the oldest U.S. tech companies – and
    their unusual histories, *Venturebeat*, 27 February [online] https://
    venturebeat.com/2014/02/27/5-of-the-oldest-u-s-tech-companies-
    and-their-unusual-histories/ (archived at https://perma.cc/
    NWR3-AZM4) [accessed 23 October 2018]

11 Collins English Dictionary (nd) Definition of 'horseless carriage'
    [online] www.collinsdictionary.com/dictionary/english/horseless-
    carriage (archived at https://perma.cc/W49S-W3KY) [accessed 10
    October 2018]

12 University College London (2008) How believing can be seeing:
    context dictates what we believe we see, *Science Daily*, 19 February
    [online] www.sciencedaily.com/releases/2008/02/080215103210.
    htm (archived at https://perma.cc/8JNV-7L2W) [accessed 10
    October 2018]

13 BBC Top Gear (nd) Top Gear's guide to: Volvo [online] www.
    topgear.com/car-reviews/find/make/volvo (archived at https://perma.
    cc/2T4S-9AQB) [accessed 10 October 2018]

14 European Commission (nd) Mobility and transport [online]
    ec.europa.eu/transport/road_safety/specialist/knowledge/vehicle/
    vehicle_safety_policy/who_regulates_vehicle_safety_en (archived at
    https://perma.cc/28Z3-SBFK) [accessed 10 October 2018]

15 Volvo Love (nd) Volvo's (many) safety innovations [online] https://
    volvoloveblog.wordpress.com/2016/01/10/volvos-many-safety-
    innovations/ (archived at https://perma.cc/S88K-EC7L) [accessed 10
    October 2018]

16 Quick MBA (nd) Marketing: Positioning [online] www.quickmba. com/marketing/ries-trout/positioning/ (archived at https://perma. cc/9GE3-AHF5) [accessed 16 October 2018]

17 Encyclopaedia Britannica (nd) Confirmation bias [online] www. britannica.com/science/confirmation-bias (archived at https://perma. cc/D2KE-FNJX) [accessed 10 October 2018]

18 Ogilvy, D (1983) *Ogilvy on Advertising*, Prion Books, Chicago

19 Oetting, J (2018) You're shameless: creative examples of agencies and their self-promotion campaigns [blog] *Hubspot*, 26 February [online] blog.hubspot.com/agency/creative-agency-self-promotion (archived at https://perma.cc/WF92-2LWZ) [accessed 11 November 2018]

20 Ogilvy, D (1972) How to create advertising that sells, *Publishing for Publicity* [online] www.publishingforpublicity.com/wp-content/ uploads/2012/04/David_Ogilvy_How_To_Create_Advertising_That_ Sells.jpg (archived at https://perma.cc/JD7H-NUFZ) [accessed 11 October 2018]

21 Maynard, N (2016) The Dove Effect: Ogilvy on positioning, Chapter 2: how to produce advertising that sells, Part II, *Medium*, 10 May [online] medium.com/ogilvy-on-digital-advertising/the-dove-effect-ogilvy-on-positioning-4a88f68c48bc (archived at https://perma.cc/ BW4Y-TD4D) [accessed 11 October 2018]

22 Tharp, P (1999) Founder of Ogilvy & Mather ad firm is dead, *New York Post*, 22 July [online] nypost.com/1999/07/22/founder-of-ogilvy-mather-ad-firm-is-dead/ (archived at https://perma.cc/ FZV7-8YEZ) [accessed 11 October 2018]

23 Maynard (2016) (see note 21 above)

24 About the Walt Disney Company [online] www.thewaltdisney-company.com/about/ (archived at https://perma.cc/K8VX-LLD6) [accessed 11 October 2018]

25 Jones, B (2018) How Disney encourages employees to deliver exceptional customer service, *Harvard Business Review*, 28 February [online] hbr.org/sponsored/2018/02/how-disney-encourages-employees-to-deliver-exceptional-customer-service (archived at https://perma.cc/P7BS-TRVF) [accessed 11 October 2018]

26 Albanesius, C (2015) Why did Google create Alphabet? *PC Magazine*, 11 August [online] uk.pcmag.com/internet-products/70295/feature/why-did-google-create-alphabet (archived at https://perma.cc/37TP-CQMM) [accessed 11 October 2018]

27 Highfield, V (2015) The 11 companies that make up Alphabet, Google: Alphabet is a set of companies, but what do they all actually do? 11/08. [online]: www.alphr.com/google/1001350/the-11-companies-that-make-up-alphabet (archived at https://perma.cc/AJ6C-ZKTN) [accessed 11 October 2018]

28 Net Market Share (2018) Search engine market share, September [online] netmarketshare.com/search-engine-market-share.aspx? (archived at https://perma.cc/WS2X-ACMG) [accessed 11 October 2018]

29 Hawkins, A J (2018) Automakers team up with states to get Americans to buy more electric cars: 'Drive Change. Drive Electric', *The Verge*, 29 March [online] www.theverge.com/2018/3/29/17173176/electric-car-marketing-campaign-automakers-northeast-states (archived at https://perma.cc/U264-NCL5) [accessed 11 October 2018]

30 Tesla (nd) Tesla's mission is to accelerate the world's transition to sustainable energy [online] www.tesla.com/en_GB/about (archived at https://perma.cc/L3D8-QX3J) [accessed 11 October 2018]

31 King, S R (1998) Making its marque at the top: Toyota's Lexus offers a lesson in brand development, *New York Times*, 21 October [online] www.nytimes.com/1998/10/21/business/making-its-marque-at-the-top-toyota-s-lexus-offers-a-lesson-in-brand-development.html (archived at https://perma.cc/E56A-PXHL) [accessed 12 October 2018]

32 Duggan, W (2018) These are the biggest and best car companies in the world, *U.S. News*, 08 May [online] money.usnews.com/investing/slideshows/the-10-most-valuable-auto-companies-in-the-world (archived at https://perma.cc/JQ76-LFVW) [accessed 11 October 2018]

VISUALS ARE THE MOST IMPORTANT ASPECT OF ANY MARKETING COMMUNICATIONS

'Since the introduction of printing,' wrote Oscar Wilde in *The Critic As Artist*, '...there has been a tendency in literature to appeal more and more to the eye, and less and less to the ear, which is really the sense which, from the stand-point of pure art, it should seek to please, and by whose canons of pleasure it should abide always' [1].

If this was true in 1891, when *The Critic As Artist* was published, it would be interesting to think what Oscar Wilde would make of the contemporary digital world where visual communications dominate. Cameras are a component of virtually every smart phone, encouraging us to capture and share images with our family, friends and wider networks. Many of today's most popular social media platforms such as Instagram, Snapchat and Pinterest are visually driven. Even on Facebook, the biggest social media platform in the world, visual content is dominant, and the world's second biggest-platform, YouTube, is a video-sharing site.

There are statistics all over the web that will testify to the power of visuals. For example, tweets with images receive 150 per cent more retweets than those without images [2]. In a study of over 1 million articles, BuzzSumo found that articles with an image once every 75–100 words achieved double the number of shares than articles with fewer images. From looking at over 100 million Facebook updates, BuzzSumo also found that updates with images had 2.3 times more engagement than those without [3].

The ubiquity of emojis means that today, even when we are writing text messages, we infuse them with images. To put this into perspective, 5 billion emojis are sent daily just on Facebook Messenger alone [4]. The evidence appears overwhelming. In a digital world, visuals do seem to be the most important aspect of effective communications.

Of course, speech is the earliest communication form known to human beings and is auditory. Is it possible that, as the web becomes increasingly awash with visuals, something as innate as language is being undervalued? After all, pictures do have the ability to communicate knowledge quickly. For example, think how much information a family holiday photograph can convey. The everyday use of signs and symbols, such as the warnings used to guide traffic on our roads, as well as instructive illustrations such as graphs and charts, prove the effectiveness of information that is depicted visually.

This kind of evidence leads people to roll out clichés such as 'a picture is worth a thousand words', but even if this were true, the scope of an illustration is limited. While pictures can get a lot of information across, text is often required to provide context and meaning to the images shown. For example, graphs, charts and infographics will normally carry a limited amount of text to provide the visuals with meaning. Moreover, the opposite is also true. Words can create a thousand images. The legend goes that Ernest Hemingway was lunching with friends and bet that he could make them cry with a story only six words long. The words written on a napkin in the restaurant read, 'For Sale: baby shoes, never worn' [5]. These mere six words have the ability to conjure up a multitude of images and emotions.

Nor should one underestimate the popularity of the spoken word. Alistair Cooke, in one of his 'Letter from America' programmes for the BBC, referred to the story of the little boy who said 'he preferred radio to television because the pictures are better' [6]. In fact, 93 per cent of adults in the United States currently listen to the radio on a weekly basis [7], as do 89.6 per cent of the UK population [8]. Online, 26 per cent of people in the United States listen to a podcast at least once a month [9] as do 23 per cent of the UK population [10], and these figures are growing.

In fact, the figures above demonstrate the power of the spoken word and language, and yet the same is not true in the reverse. If one walks away from the television during the commercials but is able to hear them, they can potentially still influence and will often make sense. Watching adverts with the sound turned down, though, will usually result in them losing a lot of their potency. Similarly, one could read a newspaper without any images. Admittedly it would not be nearly as enticing, or interesting, but it would make sense. Conversely, a newspaper with only pictures and no words would just not work.

The fact is that being able to convey ideas, concepts, value and information is inconceivable without the use of language. Explaining a new product or service and expressing the value it provides would be almost impossible in pictures alone. As Philip Sullivan points out in his book *The World According to Homo Sapiens*, 'We need words to convey our concepts'. He states, 'Words and concepts within our human information-processing equipment are as inseparable as the two sides of a coin' [11].

Indeed, language is very important for concepts to find a place in our minds. For example, if you lose a spouse, you are a widow or widower; if you lose a parent, you are an orphan. However, there is no word for a parent that has lost a child [12]. It is not that we are unable to conceive this idea, it is just that without a word, it is less likely to enter our minds. The power of a brand, and of a company having a market position, is that both exist in the mind of the customer. Without language this is unlikely to occur.

In other words, while visuals can be extremely memorable, they will lose their effectiveness if they are not connected to a verbal idea. As Al Ries and Jack Trout articulated in their book *Positioning: The battle for your mind*: 'Pictures alone won't build a position in the mind. Only words will do that. To create an effective positioning programme, you have to verbalize the visuals' [13].

Whether brands become identified with a category, or a single idea, there needs to be a verbal element to the communication. So, for many people, ketchup is synonymous with Heinz, safety with Volvo, search with Google, Disney with theme parks and Nike with athletic performance. It is not enough that these brands have powerful visual identities. We also need to be able to verbalize what they are about.

The importance of words is also why names matter. As Jack Trout pointed out, 'Would "Alfred" perfume have sold as well as "Charlie"? And Hog Island in the Caribbean was going nowhere until its name was changed to Paradise Island' [14].

The power of language and names is becoming ever more critical in a world of 'conversational commerce'. Digital assistants such as Apple's Siri, Amazon's Alexa, Microsoft's Cortana and Google's Assistant are becoming increasingly popular. Voice search is a growing trend and it is estimated that by 2020, 50 per cent of all searches will be undertaken by voice [15]. The increasing popularity of audio-centric devices such as Amazon's Echo and Google's Home means that in the same year, 30 per cent of web browsing sessions will be performed without a screen [16]. This means that there are likely to be times when buyers will solely be using language to search, describe needs, articulate challenges and recall brands. Companies that own language, within their market sector, will have a distinct advantage over competitors.

Language, of course, has the ability to create sensory experiences for the reader or listener by describing sight, touch, taste, smell and sound. As the great poet Sylvia Plath wrote:

The artist's life nourishes itself on the particular, the concrete. . . Start with the mat-green fungus in the pine woods yesterday: words about it, describing it, and a poem will come. . . Write about the cow, Mrs. Spaulding's heavy eyelids, the smell of vanilla flavouring in a brown bottle. That's where the magic mountains begin' [17].

In an article for *Adage*, Al Ries points out the importance of using visual words. He explains that the power of Zappos offering free shipping is that it can be instantly visualized. Similarly, BMW's slogan 'The ultimate driving machine' is another example. BMW could have used the slogan 'The ultimate performance machine', but driving can be visualized, and performance cannot. Al Ries observes that we call a table that holds all drinks a coffee table, not a beverage table, because coffee is a word that can be visualized. Likewise, we take a suitcase on trips, not a clothing case, because a suit is a visual word [18].

While the power of language is sometimes neglected in our visually driven digital world, the fact is that both visuals and language are important in marketing communications. The majority of the greatest and most successful brands utilize both effectively.

For example, Apple has a memorable and easily identifiable logo. At the same time, its 'Think different' slogan from the 1990s has stuck and helped position the brand in the customer's mind. Similarly, everyone is familiar with the Coca-Cola logo and its iconic glass bottle. However, the use of straplines, perhaps most famously 'It's the real thing', have played an important part in its success. From Nike's 'swoosh' logo and strapline 'Just Do It' to L'Oréal's use of imagery and 'Because I'm worth it' tag, the greatest brands combine the use of visuals and language to create the most powerful communications.

Ultimately, this is borne out by what we know about how human beings learn. Linda Kreger Silverman, an author and licensed psychologist, explains that about 33 per cent of people primarily think in pictures, 25 per cent primarily think in words and 45 per cent rely on both hemispheres [19]. Consequently, the ineffective use of language or visuals in communications severely limits the potency of the media. Ultimately, it is the combination of visuals and language that provides companies and brands with the greatest chance of creating memorable and influential messaging.

Notes

1 Wilde, O (1891) *The Critic as Artist* (*Upon the Importance of Doing Nothing and Discussing Everything*), Mondial, New York

2 Cooper, B B (2016) How Twitter's expanded images increase clicks, retweets and favorites, *Buffer*, 27 April [online] blog.bufferapp.com/the-power-of-twitters-new-expanded-images-and-how-to-make-the-most-of-it (archived at https://perma.cc/539V-BGTG) [accessed 05 November 2018]

3 Pinantoan, A (2015) How to massively boost your blog traffic with these 5 awesome image stats, *BuzzSumo*, 20 May [online] buzzsumo.com/blog/how-to-massively-boost-your-blog-traffic-with-these-5-awesome-image-stats/ (archived at https://perma.cc/LDZ4-XV2Q) [accessed 05 November 2018]

4 Emojipedia (nd) Emoji Statistics [online] emojipedia.org/stats/ (archived at https://perma.cc/FL4G-PL79) [accessed 05 November 2018]

5 Lehman, D (2014) The shortest story ever told, *The American Scholar*, 28 October [online] theamericanscholar.org/the-shortest-story-ever-told/#.W8WHshMzaqA (archived at https://perma.cc/65BP-UVM5) [accessed 05 November 2018]

6 Cooke, A (1985) Letter from America by Alistair Cooke: US farming in crisis, *BBC*, 15 February [online] www.bbc.co.uk/programmes/articles/5v9nnbGDNYYrmvjn2BlNcNf/us-farming-in-crisis (archived at https://perma.cc/WX7B-DTZL) [accessed 05 November 2018]

7 Nielsen (2018) How America listens: the American audio landscape [online] https://www.nielsen.com/us/en/insights/article/2018/

how-america-listens-the-american-audio-landscape/ (archived at https://perma.cc/RB47-V6XU) [accessed 05 November 2018]

8 Ofcom (2017) Communications Market Report 2017 – United Kingdom [online] www.ofcom.org.uk/__data/assets/pdf_file/0014/105440/uk-radio-audio.pdf (archived at https://perma.cc/L2C2-PMDG) [accessed 05 November 2018]

9 Podcast Insights (2018) 2018 podcast stats & facts (new research from June 2018) [online] www.podcastinsights.com/podcast-statistics/ (archived at https://perma.cc/HRQ6-GHHN) [accessed 05 November 2018]

10 Hebblethwaite, C (2018) 23% of UK population listened to a podcast in the last month, *Marketing Tech News*, 29 March [online] www.marketingtechnews.net/news/2018/mar/29/23-uk-population-listened-podcast-last-month/ (archived at https://perma.cc/C5F5-RFCL) [accessed 05 November 2018]

11 Sullivan, P R (2005) *The World According to Homo Sapiens: (or Why We Humans Experience the World ...* iUniverse, Lincoln

12 Belkin, L (2010) Motherload: describing grief [blog] *New York Times*, 08 June [online] parenting.blogs.nytimes.com/2010/06/08/describing-grief/ (archived at https://perma.cc/DQ65-B6JT) [accessed 05 November 2018]

13 Ries, A and Trout, J (2000) *Positioning: The battle for your mind*, McGraw-Hill, New York

14 Trout, J (2005) The brain's ear for info, *Forbes*, 24 October [online] www.forbes.com/2005/10/19/marketing-advertising-communicating-cx_jt_1024trout_comm05.html#3bb3cd393530 (archived at https://perma.cc/P6B9-VBZ6) [accessed 05 November 2018]

15 Olson, C (2016) Just say it: the future of search is voice and personal digital assistants, *Campaign*, 25 April [online] www.campaignlive.co.uk/article/just-say-it-future-search-voice-personal-digital-assistants/1392459 (archived at https://perma.cc/T6TK-T8GN) [accessed 05 November 2018]

16 Gartner (2016) Gartner reveals top predictions for IT organizations and users in 2017 and beyond [online] www.gartner.com/newsroom/id/3482117 (archived at https://perma.cc/N3PA-8CTP) [accessed 05 November 2018]

17 Kukil, K V (2000) *The Unabridged Journals of Sylvia Plath 1950–1962, ed. Karen V Kukil*, Anchor, New York

18 Ries, A (2017) What's missing in most marketing programs? Verbal imagery, *Ad Age*, 13 February [online] adage.com/article/al-ries/missing-marketing-programs-verbal-imagery/307915/ (archived at https://perma.cc/B3XM-RTFJ) [accessed 05 November 2018]

19 Kreger Silverman PhD, L (2005) Upside-down brilliance: the visual-spatial learner, *The Institute for the Study of Advanced Development*, 24 November [online] www.pegy.org.uk/Upside-Down%20 Brilliance%20-A4%20pdf.pdf (archived at https://perma.cc/JW3S-QDF8) [accessed 05 November 2018]

MYTH

17

OUR OFFERING MUST ATTRACT THE LARGEST AUDIENCE POSSIBLE

If the essence of strategy, as the business academic Michael Porter once stated, is 'choosing what not to do' [1], then many businesses don't have a marcom strategy at all. In any market there is the 'Total Addressable Market', that is the overall revenue opportunity available if 100 per cent market share is achieved [2].

So, three IT engineers, starting a new business, may assess the Total Addressable Market as any enterprise that has IT requirements throughout the world. Of course, these three engineers have no scope to service a global market. Consequently, they may decide that realistically they can only service organizations within a 50-mile radius of their offices. This would become their 'Serviceable Available Market', the market segment actually within the company's reach [3].

For many businesses this is as much segmentation as they undertake. The thinking is often that because the company can service any organization within this 50-mile radius, why exclude any enterprise and limit potential opportunities? This approach is fundamentally flawed.

In order to ensure the IT business appeals to the diverse nature of organizations within a 50-mile radius of its offices, it has to keep its communications very general. Subsequently, its messages are bland and unable to stand out or appeal to anyone in particular. This renders them ineffective.

Conversely, if this IT company chose only to market to law firms it would alienate the overwhelming majority of enterprises in the area. However, its messaging and the content it could produce would address particular issues facing law firms. It could reference software and products that they regularly use and utilize imagery that is likely to feel relevant and appeal to this target audience.

By being able to be specific, talk their language and address pertinent issues within the sector, it is more probable that the content will be applicable and engaging and really obtain some audience attention.

In addition to this, the IT company would have more of a chance of differentiating itself amongst the plethora of other suppliers in the market. While offering IT solutions to any organization might mean it is up against hundreds of other enterprises, once it specializes within the legal market, it may find that it has far fewer direct competitors.

Differentiation does not often come from what a company does. After all, servicing a customer's IT requirements requires certain skillsets and approaches that will be identical whichever expert provides the service. Today, enterprises will often differentiate by 'how' they deliver the service.

By focusing on the legal market, a company will be able to design an approach that fits the working habits, culture and expectations of law firms. While the actual IT expertise offered may be similar to most competitors, the service delivery may be distinctive. Differentiation goes beyond the product itself, as can be seen with a company such as Apple, where you don't just buy a computer or a phone, but a seamless array of related online services and a genius bar to help you solve problems. Similarly, when purchasing items from IKEA, you don't just buy a couch or a cabinet, but a means of decision making, assembly, and delivery [4].

In choosing this particular market segment, it will also be more obvious which channels to market are likely to be most effective in reaching lawyers. There will be certain online forums, networks and platforms they use, societies and associations to which they belong, events they attend and commercial interests they follow. All of these considerations increase the likelihood that the communications will have a positive impact.

Concentrating marketing efforts on a smaller segment is likely to lead to a company getting much more 'bang for its buck' from its marcom activities. If this IT company decides its marketplace is any business within a 50-mile radius of its offices then its communications might find its way to a recruitment firm on the southern edge of its geographical region, a manufacturing business 100 miles away at the northern tip of its area and a doctor's surgery in the middle. Communicating to very different businesses, considerable distances away from each other, is unlikely to enable the IT company to build much awareness within the market.

Alternatively, only concentrating on law firms within a certain locality means targeting a more cohesive group. Many of these lawyers will know each other, network at particular conferences, belong to the same societies and associations, and utilize similar communication channels. This will make it much more probable that, over time, this IT company can become known and build a positive reputation.

It is often helpful to think of target market segments in terms of communities. The *Oxford English Dictionary* defines a community as 'a group of people with shared values and/or interests' [5]. If a business identifies these values and interests within the context of its offering, it is much more probable that it will create messaging and communications that prospects will find relevant, interesting and engaging. This is likely to lead to more opportunities and business.

The main reason that organizations don't segment down to smaller markets is that they are concerned with excluding opportunities. Many company leaders feel that trying to appeal to the largest possible audience provides the most chances to win business. What they fail to realize is that unless they have the available resources to reach everyone within their Serviceable Available Market then they are already segmenting. Rather than undertaking this segmentation in a strategic manner they are simply doing it by running out of time and money.

Strategically, a company should focus on the smallest market it can that is big enough to ensure it can realistically hit its commercial targets. An enterprise should think of this as the 'Smallest Viable Market'. So, if our IT start-up's first milestone is to have 100 clients, segmenting a marketplace containing 10,000 companies would mean it would only have to win 1 per cent of the business to achieve it aims. In this scenario, and with a small marketing resource, why would it try to communicate with a bigger segment and in so doing dilute the potency of the communications it creates?

No matter what stage of development an organization is at, it makes complete sense for an enterprise to spend its money on the people most likely to buy. Concentrating its offering, service delivery and marketing communications on a focused group, or groups, makes it easier to create a compelling proposition that will attract the customers it wants and enable the business to attain commercial success.

As a company grows, it can always enter new segments, as long as the brand narrative makes sense. In other words, an organization needs to be able to communicate why it has the competency to bring its expertise to another market in a way that feels right to customers. For example, Facebook started as a platform specifically for Harvard students. With 50 per cent of students signed up in its first month [6], it was rolled out to Stanford, Yale and Colombia [7], all of which are in the top 10 universities in the United States. By the end of 2004, Facebook was being used by most universities in the United States and Canada [8].

In September 2005, high school students could join Facebook, along with employees from Microsoft and Apple. It continued to expand into universities and high schools in Australia, New Zealand, Mexico, Ireland and the UK. Membership was only opened up to the general public, over 13 years old, in September 2006 [8]. Today, Facebook has well over 2 billion monthly active users [9]. If it had started life as a platform for everyone, it is unlikely it would have been able to penetrate any market and survive.

Similarly, Jeff Bezos always desired that Amazon would be an everything store. He wanted to build an internet company that would be an intermediary between manufacturers and customers and sell almost all products. Of course, as a start-up, it would have been impossible for Amazon to sell 'everything'. Instead, it would have ended up with a random array of products with no obvious target market. So, Amazon focused on books.

By choosing books, Jeff Bezos immediately had a compelling value proposition. While there were 3 million active books in print in 1994, when Amazon started, the largest bookstores only stocked about 150,000 [10]. Amazon could immediately offer a greater selection of titles than any physical retail outlet. The product also provided Bezos with an obvious target market of avid readers and book lovers.

Once it had built a good reputation as a credible online retailer for books, Amazon could then start to offer other products. The very next category it went into was compact discs. From a brand narrative perspective this works. For customers, if an online store can deliver books reliably it is not difficult to believe that it can also supply CDs, a not dissimilar product. Expanding its market to book and music lovers still meant it had a definite target audience on which to focus. Providing books and CDs enabled Amazon to become the most successful merchant on the internet. It then started to diversify its product offering through acquisition of other businesses.

Likewise, Red Bull today is one of the top 10 soft drinks manu-facturers in the world [11]. In 1987, launching a new product into a mature Western drinks market was not easy. How does a small business compete with global giants such as Coca-Cola, PepsiCo and Unilever?

The answer is that a small business can compete with even the biggest enterprises if it concentrates its efforts on a very narrow market rather than try to attract the largest audience possible.

Dietrich Mateschitz, the Founder of Red Bull, began focusing solely on students. He paid students and DJs to host parties where the drink was served [12]. Creating a buzz and demand amongst students gave Red Bull a base from which to grow. Even now, Red Bull's target market is students and young professionals [13]. It is being this focused, rather than trying to appeal to the largest audience possible, which enables it to have a strong brand image and keep its appeal.

While trying to make a company attractive to the largest audience possible seems like the safest strategy to deliver commercial success, the opposite is in fact true. Attempting to be all things to all people actually results in a business being nothing to anyone. Rather, by focusing on a target group an enterprise can develop an offering, delivery and communications that are compelling for that particular market segment. Having a razor-sharp focus on the target market is vital for any business to be successful. No matter how small or large the organization, it is knowing exactly who its customers are, and ensuring it delivers for them, that will be the key to its prosperity.

Notes

1 Magretta, J (2011) Strategic Planning – Jim Collins, Meet Michael Porter, *Harvard Business Review*, 15 December [online] hbr.org/2011/12/jim-collins-meet-michael-porte (archived at https://perma.cc/5B9R-Q3KQ) [accessed 25 December 2018]

2 Corporate Finance Institute (nd) What is the Total Addressable Market (TAM)? [online] corporatefinanceinstitute.com/resources/knowledge/strategy/total-addressable-market-tam/ (archived at https://perma.cc/D4UK-TV3S) [accessed 25 December 2018]

3 Corporate Finance Institute (nd) What is the Total Addressable Market (TAM)? [online] corporatefinanceinstitute.com/resources/knowledge/strategy/total-addressable-market-tam/ (archived at https://perma.cc/D4UK-TV3S) [accessed 25 December 2018]

4 Leinwand, P and Mainardi, C (2016) Your whole company needs to be distinctive, not just your product, *Harvard Business Review*, 19 May [online] hbr.org/2016/05/your-whole-company-needs-to-be-distinctive-not-just-your-product (archived at https://perma.cc/GG2Y-3RCJ) [accessed 25 December 2018]

5 English Oxford Living Dictionaries (nd) Definition of community in English [online] en.oxforddictionaries.com/definition/community (archived at https://perma.cc/2QEC-9BGX) [accessed 25 December 2018]

6 Boyd, J (2018) The history of Facebook: from BASIC to global giant, *Brandwatch*, 05 February [online] www.brandwatch.com/blog/history-of-facebook/ (archived at https://perma.cc/KFB9-TR7B) [accessed 25 January 2018]

7 Barr, S (2018) When did Facebook start? The story behind a company that took over the world, *Independent*, 23 August [online] www.independent.co.uk/life-style/gadgets-and-tech/facebook-when-started-how-mark-zuckerberg-history-harvard-eduardo-saverin-a8505151.html (archived at https://perma.cc/59LN-32D5) [accessed 25 December 2018]

8 Boyd (2018) (see note 6 above)

9 Statista (2018) Number of monthly active Facebook users worldwide as of 3rd quarter 2018 (in millions) [online] www.statista.com/statistics/264810/number-of-monthly-active-facebook-users-worldwide/ (archived at https://perma.cc/F7P5-ZXA5) [accessed 25 December 2018]

10 Kozlowski, M (2018) Amazon CEO Jeff Bezos talks about selling books in new interview [blog] *Good E Reader*, 09 May [online] goodereader.com/blog/business-news/

amazon-ceo-jeff-bezos-talks-about-selling-books-in-new-interview (archived at https://perma.cc/6WST-LSVC) [accessed 25 December 2018]

11 adbrands (2018) The world's leading non-alcoholic drinks companies ranked by revenues [online] www.adbrands.net/sectors/sector-soft-drinks.htm (archived at https://perma.cc/X2ZE-9P6V) [accessed 26 December 2018]

12 Arlidge, J (2004) How Red Bull woke up the teen market, *Guardian*, 05 December [online] www.theguardian.com/media/2004/dec/05/advertising.formulaone (archived at https://perma.cc/9M34-ALM7) [accessed 26 December 2018]

13 Dudovskiy, J (2016) Red Bull segmentation, targeting and positioning, *Research Methodology*, 28 June [online] research-methodology.net/red-bull-segmentation-targeting-positioning/ (archived at https://perma.cc/Q4H7-LU52) [accessed 26 December 2018]

MYTH
18

DEMOGRAPHY IS THE BEST WAY TO SEGMENT YOUR MARKET

Market segmentation is the process of dividing up the potential market into distinct groups. These segments will either have the same requirements, or behave in a similar way, in relation to a company's offering. To be of value, the separate categories of customer must be sufficiently different to warrant a specific strategy.

Segmenting the market enables enterprises to create offerings and communications that are relevant and most likely to resonate with the target customer. It allows a business to focus its limited resources on a particular group, or groups, of buyers that are more prone to make a purchase. In this way, an organization increases its chances of success.

The most common form of market segmentation is demographic [1]. This is made up of social characteristics such as:

- age – year of birth as well as generational;
- gender;
- sexual orientation;
- education;

- income;
- occupation;
- socio-economic status;
- religion;
- ethnicity;
- nationality;
- family structure/lifecycle – eg married, single, retired etc;
- family size;
- geography – variable categories such as urban, suburban, rural, wealthy/poor areas etc.

Any number of these categories could be relevant depending on the offering a company wants to promote. A restaurant will most likely make use of geographic segmentation as there is only a certain distance that the majority of people will be willing to travel for a meal. An expensive luxury hotel might choose to target individuals from a particular socio-economic group, as it is probable that they will be able to afford to stay. Manufacturers of seven-seater vehicles could decide that one target group should be families of a particular size, and at a certain stage in life, as they will require the prerequisite number of seats.

While demography can be a useful starting point for segmentation it is severely limited in its scope. For example, consider two males born in 1948 and raised in England. Both have been married twice, have children, are successful, wealthy and like dogs. Yet one of these is Prince Charles and the other is the Prince of Darkness, Ozzy Osbourne, the lead singer of Black Sabbath. Although they have a considerable number of demographic characteristics in common, one would imagine that they have very different criteria in many of the purchases they make.

Similarly, millennials are frequently referred to as if they are a cohesive demographic group. Generalizations are often made about this generation such as, 'they value personal development over financial benefits', or they 'embrace sustainability'. Yet making these conjectures about a group that numbers 73 million individuals in the United States alone [2] is hugely simplistic and likely to prove inaccurate. It is dubious that demography by itself will deliver the robust insights on which an effective marketing strategy can be based.

This is compounded by the idea of post-demographic consumerism which highlights the fact that in an age where access to information and brands is ubiquitous, and people have the ability to experiment more than in previous eras using digital technology, the traditional demographic models of consumer behaviour are becoming less relevant. In 2015, Netflix vice president of product innovation Todd Yellin described traditional demographics as 'almost useless'. He continued: 'Because... there are actually 19-year-old guys who watch *Dance Moms*, and there are 73-year-old women who are watching *Breaking Bad* and *Avengers*' [3].

The same can be said of 'firmographics', which are for companies what demographics are for people. Characteristics distinguished by firmographics are:

- date established/years in business;
- sector;
- number of employees;
- locations (geography and number of offices);
- revenue/turnover;
- ownership (public, private, government, not for profit);
- market share/industry position;
- customers (B2B, B2C).

As with demographics, firmographics are quite limited in scope. Consider two bars, both established in 1998 with 25 mostly part-time employees and located in the same city. Both have similar revenues, are owner managed and serve the public. Although according to the firmographics they might be the same, the culture and attitude of the businesses may be very different. This will affect their views on risk, investment, how they run the bar and consequently purchasing.

While firmographics may be a useful starting point in identifying target market segments, as with demography, both are incomplete and unsatisfactory as a way of segmenting a market if used in isolation. Other factors should be considered when categorizing the market, in order to make the groups more meaningful and provide businesses with a greater chance of success.

Behavioural segmentation classifies the market on buying behaviours or preferences. It is an important consideration as it forces an organization to ask many questions that are likely to make its marketing communications more effective. Behavioural segmentation can be extremely complex. This is especially true when interpreting purchasing behaviour online, when the links that are clicked, the information that is looked at and the overall buying journey can be analysed with a view to improving the user experience and conversion rates.

There are, I believe, four core areas that should be examined when using behavioural segmentation.

1 Benefits sought/challenges resolved

A good question to ask is, 'What are the challenges that a prospect is trying to solve that may lead them to our offering?' So, in a B2B environment, an IT services supplier may understand that one of the possible challenges its prospects have is around data. The issue may be, 'How do I collect, store and analyse data in the most effective and secure way?' Another concern may be related to competitive advantage or, 'How do I keep up with market trends and make sure that I don't miss out to competitors?'

Similarly, in the consumer world, the seller of a luxury car may be answering questions such as, 'How do I demonstrate my success?' or 'How do I reward myself for a particular achievement, or on reaching a specific milestone?'

Thinking in terms of challenges is useful as it facilitates putting yourself in your buyers' position and contemplating what motivates them to buy. The other side of this coin is to consider the offering in terms of benefits sought. So, in the case of our IT company, one of the benefits, in the scenarios above, was the ability to collect, keep and utilize data more effectively. In the case of the luxury car, it was the reward for an achievement.

Of course, buyers can have more than one motivation to purchase at a time. Segmenting the market by these different motivations may make articulating the offering easier, could mean that certain channels to market become more appropriate and can enable the targeting of prospects to be undertaken more efficiently and with greater success.

2 Occasion/context of the purchase

Almost every purchase is triggered by an event. Thinking in terms of the contexts or events that lead to buying can be extremely useful:

- *Universal occasions* – an accountancy practice may know that the end of the financial year is a good time to target business owners who are unhappy with their financial results. A flower store can promote its offering leading up to Valentine's Day, Mother's Day etc. Pizza delivery companies might run promotions around big sporting events such as the Olympics, World Cup or Super Bowl when they know people will sit at home and snack while watching.

- *Recurring personal occasions* – companies may have specific times of year when they run particular training programmes, set business strategy or review suppliers. There may be regular business trips that take place every quarter. Similarly, individuals will have certain birthdays and anniversaries that they celebrate every year. There can even be daily purchases such as a cup of coffee on the way to work.

- *Singular occasions* – there are rare or infrequent events that nevertheless will be the trigger for a purchase. Starting a new business might be the reason an individual looks for an accountant. A pregnancy might lead a growing family to look for a bigger vehicle. A wedding could lead to the hiring of a photographer.

A company that understands the context in which purchases take place can choose to target and message using this as a framework. While the circumstances of a purchase have always been relevant, in a world where customers are empowered to go online and look for suppliers themselves, producing messaging, promotions and content that directly address context can be extremely effective.

This is even more pertinent in a world driven by mobile smart devices. Google speaks of 'micro moments'; these are 'intent-driven moments of decision making and preference shaping that occur throughout the entire consumer journey'. They happen instantaneously and spontaneously and will often be driven by the context in which purchasers find themselves. Segmenting by context can directly address these 'micro-moments' [4].

3 Usage

How much a product or service is used could be the basis for segmenting a market. There will be heavy, medium and light users of different products and services. For example, a business traveller embarking on over 20 long-haul return flights per year and spending 100 nights in hotels, will probably be considered a heavy user of air travel and hotels. Another business traveller flying eight times per year and spending 30 nights in hotels may be thought of as a medium user. Meanwhile, an individual who only books one or two business flights per year together with a short hotel stay, may be perceived as a light user. This degree of usage may alter the criteria used to make a purchase in areas such as expectations, convenience and other specific requirements.

4 Loyalty

Allegiance to a particular company or brand can be a useful way of segmenting a market. Companies can choose to reward their most loyal customers with points, rewards, vouchers and privileges etc, as frequently undertaken by airlines, hotels and supermarkets. Similarly, a business may choose to target customers of a particular competitor. It could be the brand has had a difficult time or the business feels it has some real competitive advantage and a superior offering.

While behavioural segmentation might provide an organization with some interesting opportunities, a company may also want to consider psychographic segmentation. This is undertaken by understanding the activities, interests and opinions (AIOs) of prospects. Different information will be relevant depending on the offering of the enterprise. Particular businesses will choose to focus on certain aspects of a psychographic profile:

Activities – the actions someone takes. For example, they may take the train to work every day, visit the gym three times per week, regularly attend the cinema and theatre and attend church every Sunday morning.

Interests – an individual may have an affection for family, cooking and collecting old vinyl records. Another could be passionate about technology, politics and fashion.

Opinions – of course people have an array of points of view about many different subjects. Particular beliefs may be pertinent for certain organizations. So, views about specific public figures, brands or films, political beliefs and certain values may be relevant depending on the offering a company provides.

While utilizing psychographics may not be as straightforward as demography, there are a number of ways an organization can make use of this information. For example, an investment business may understand that its higher risk, higher returns offering appeals to an individual with a certain propensity for risk. The nature of the investments might also mean that it is easier to sell to someone with a particular political outlook. With this in mind, the company could utilize messaging that is more likely to appeal to this type of person and will most probably turn off other individuals. The better an enterprise understands its market, the bolder it can be with its communications. This will enable it to increasingly appeal to the very people that it wants to attract.

A high-end sports fashion company may decide that individuals who regularly visit the gym are a good target for its clothing. It may use this psychographic information together with demographic categorization. In this way it will target specific geographical locations that are more likely to contain gym members with the appropriate financial profile for the brand. The fashion company may be able to partner with specific gyms, in the right locations, in order to obtain access to their members.

The use of social platforms and digital media has meant that significant numbers of individuals are leaving digital footprints which can be used to target people psychographically. This can be combined with demographic information and even behavioural segmentation to create some really specific target groups. There are a number of ways psychographic information can be collected and obtained today including [5]:

- traditional focus groups/interviews;
- set-top box viewing data;
- surveys/questionnaires/quizzes;
- search engines/website analytics (eg Google Analytics);
- browsing data;
- social media (ie likes, clicks, tweets, posts, etc);

- third-party analytics;
- photo galleries.

For example, a vehicle manufacturer launching a new electric car would be able to target individuals who drive to work, have an interest in technology and think that more needs to be done to protect the environment. This, together with some demographic information, may enable a company to target its most probable early adopters with communications that are very likely to resonate.

While demography is a useful and accessible first layer of segmentation, it is easy to understand that it falls short of being singularly the best way of categorizing a market. While beneficial, demography must be combined with other categorizations in order to allow organizations to address prospect groups in the most relevant and appropriate manner. In so doing, this will increase the likelihood of them being successful.

Notes

1 Course Hero (nd) The most common form of consumer market segmentation [online] www.coursehero.com/file/p2arn59/The-most-common-form-of-consumer-market-segmentation-is-a-geographic-b-product/ (archived at https://perma.cc/P78J-YHNE) [accessed 27 December 2018]

2 Fry, R (2018) Millennials projected to overtake Baby Boomers as America's largest generation, *Pew Research Center* [online] www.pewresearch.org/fact-tank/2018/03/01/millennials-overtake-baby-boomers/ (archived at https://perma.cc/LHU6-BU8C) [accessed 30 December 2019]

3 Coleman, R (2015) Trends 2016: post-demographic, *Campaign*, 24 November [online] www.campaignlive.co.uk/article/trends-2016-post-demographic/1374257 (archived at https://perma.cc/86V2-MFFN) [accessed 30 December 2018]

4 Google (2015) How micro-moments are changing the rules [online] www.thinkwithgoogle.com/marketing-resources/micro-moments/

how-micromoments-are-changing-rules/ (archived at https://perma.
cc/95HR-3BCH) [accessed 30 December 2018)

5 CB Insights (2018) What is psychographics? Understanding the 'dark
arts' of marketing that brought down Cambridge Analytica [online]
www.cbinsights.com/research/what-is-psychographics/ (archived at
https://perma.cc/287Q-6KAU) [accessed 30 December 2018]

THE FOCUS OF MARKETING COMMUNICATIONS SHOULD BE A COMPANY'S PRODUCTS OR SERVICES

Imagine your customer is a hitchhiker. As you pull over and wind down the window, you tell them all about the model of car that you chose and its reliability. You then speak about your own driving experience and how they are in safe hands with you at the wheel. Finally, you talk about the music that you are playing, throughout your journey, and why you have picked certain tracks for specific times during the excursion.

If they were not so desperate for a ride, they would have walked away long before you finished speaking. This was because they wanted to start the conversation with only one question: 'Where are you going?' At that moment, their first priority was to get closer to their final destination. Any other considerations were secondary.

This is exactly how many businesses approach their marcom. They ask questions of themselves such as 'Who are we?', 'What are we good at?' and 'What benefit does that provide to customers?' They then spend time, money and energy communicating this information to their prospects.

The problem is that if a company's starting point for its communications is itself, however it massages the messaging along the way in order to appeal to a customer, it will always come back to the source. In other words, ultimately the statements will all be about the company itself. It may well end up producing communications that do not really engage customers at all.

The focus of any communications should not be the company or the products and services it offers. Rather, it should all be about the customer. An enterprise should ask, 'What are the challenges a customer will face, that might mean they consider the solutions we offer?' For example, an HR outsourcing company may understand that the challenges its prospects have are questions such as, 'How do I attract talent to my organization?', 'How do I retain my employees?', 'How do I ensure I am compliant with current legislation?', 'How do I minimize any risks when things go wrong?' and 'How do I protect my reputation?' It is these topics that represent the buying motivations of potential new customers.

In addition, a secondary query a business must ask is, 'What are the contexts in which these challenges are likely to occur?' In other words, what are the events taking place that give rise to these issues? So, in the case of our HR consultancy, examples of events may be: the company is growing and requires more employees; some key individuals have left the organization; there has been a difficult incident with a member of staff; or an occurrence has highlighted that the business is not fully compliant with current legislation. By focusing on the events and challenges that prospects are likely to encounter, an enterprise will ensure that its communications are not about the company, or its product and services, but rather its target market and their challenges, situation, hopes, fears, dreams and objectives.

While this should always have been the case, digital technology has compounded this necessity. With access to more information and choice than ever before, buyers are increasingly starting their purchase journeys online and going well over halfway through the buying journey before they get a possible supplier involved [1], if they ever do. Customers today are more proactive in their search for products and services than they were previously, when they would have conversations with customer service representatives in retail outlets, or, in the B2B world, schedule meetings in order to understand what exactly was on offer.

The further a company goes to ensure its target market is at the heart and centre of all the communications it creates, the greater the chance that its messaging will resonate and be effective. Rather than focusing on its own product and services, the mantra that any person responsible for communications should use is, 'Make our customer the hero'. Messaging that focuses on customers and their fears, challenges, aspirations and experiences will be more compelling.

Domino's Pizza does this incredibly well with its *Pizza Legends* website [2]. It allows users to create their own pizza, name it and share it. It generates a unique animation based on their individual choices and of course lets them order it as well. Customers are at the front and centre of everything about this offering.

Dove is another example of enabling its customers to be the heroes. Over the years, its self-esteem project [3] has focused on real-life stories and on the challenges that everyday people have with self-perception. Its portal provides a wealth of advice and guidance on encouraging young people to grow up with both confidence and self-esteem.

This approach does not only apply in business-to-consumer marketing. For example, in the business-to-business world, GE communicated to potential employees and customers alike through a character named 'Owen', who struggles to explain to his friends and family the significance of landing a job at GE. In this series of adverts, Owen, an everyday college graduate, is the 'hero' rather than GE itself. It is through this character that GE attempts to change the perception potential employees and customers have about the company [4].

One of the major ways that information is disseminated online is through 'social sharing'. This affects the content we consume. For example, while around two-thirds of adults in the United States get some of their news from social media [5], the challenge is that what people are exposed to depends, to a great extent, on the interest and behaviour of those with whom they connect via this medium [6]. Thus, one of the keys to being successful online is for an organization to ensure that the material it creates is shared. In this way a business can ensure it gets in front of a greater number of people, and generate more awareness about its offering.

It has been demonstrated that overall it is the material that elicits an emotional reaction that receives most exposure. Anger-inducing content is more likely to be shared than sadness-inducing content because it produces greater emotional arousal. Material that stimulates positive emotions is more widely shared than that which elicits negative feelings. Ideally, content should trigger emotions like anger, anxiety or awe and, if possible, it should be positive [7].

It is unlikely that most companies will be able to convey much emotion when creating material solely about the products and services they offer. Once they make 'their customer the hero' and ensure that the customer is at the centre of any communications, it will be easier to ensure that the content contains a necessary emotional element.

When it comes to content sharing, it is also material containing practical information that is most likely to be shared [8]. This makes sense in light of how digital has transformed the landscape for marketing communications. Marcom used to be transactional in nature; a business would pay a media organization to momentarily grab the eyes and ears of its target audience. By paying to appear on a billboard, in a magazine, on TV and radio or to be put through the postbox etc, a company could get its offering in front of potential buyers.

The fleeting nature of all these different communications meant that an enterprise would try to convey some of the key benefits of its product and service, and then entice buyers with a 'call to action' or some sort of offer. This resulted in the focus of the vast majority of marcoms being on the products and services a business supplied.

This singular approach is no longer appropriate. Whereas the channels that businesses utilized belonged to other organizations, today, routes to market such as a website, Facebook page, YouTube channel and LinkedIn profile etc, are owned by companies themselves. Media works by building an audience and then making sure it is retained. While enterprises can pay to garner attention on these platforms in order to 'get noticed', these channels will only be effective if a business can continue to build and keep the number of visitors that it receives from its target market.

If a company's media channels only deliver information about the benefits of its products and services, it is unlikely anybody will visit them more than once or twice. In order to encourage people to engage more regularly, these channels have to provide value. That is, the content has to give insights, hints, tips and other useful information that will be beneficial and interesting, even if a prospect is currently not in the market to make a purchase. So, for example, my own website, stickymarketing.com, contains hundreds of videos providing insights about marketing, communications and other related topics. It is not necessary for an individual to be interested in hiring a consultant or speaker on marketing to find the website of use.

This does not mean that a business cannot explain what it does, include calls to action or create special offers to entice prospects to buy on any of the channels it chooses to utilize. It is simply a recognition that without ensuring there is inherent value in their communications, organizations will fail to realize the potential of owning their own media.

This means that marcom is no longer a means to an end, existing simply to elicit a response which may or may not result in a sale. Marketing communications should be thought of by any business as a product in its own right. It should be used to continually build and retain an audience of its target prospects. This will provide any enterprise with one of the most vital assets in existence today – the attention of its marketplace.

In many ways, marketing communications can now be thought of as a complementary good to the actual product or service that the company sells to make a profit. This is not new. For example, the *Michelin Guide* was originally conceived by brothers Andre and Edouard Michelin to help motorists develop their trips and in turn boost car sales and, consequently, tyre purchases [9]. What was a novelty back in the early 20th century has now become a necessity in a world where every business finds itself owning media channels.

If a business focuses its communications on its products or services, it is unlikely to create material that connects emotionally with prospects. Failure to achieve this makes it less likely that its marketing will be shared. This means missing out on one of the most effective routes to market available today. Without focusing on creating value, it is unlikely that any communications will truly engage prospects. Marketing is now a product in its own right. Consequently, merely describing products and services, together with their benefits, is likely to miss the mark in this digital age.

For companies to give themselves the greatest opportunity for their communications to have a positive impact, the focus of all messaging should be the customer and their challenges, hopes, dreams and ambitions. In so doing, the material a business creates has the best chance of penetrating customers on an emotional level – a prerequisite for success. If an enterprise can avoid making its communications about its product and services but instead can focus on 'making its customers the heroes', then it has a better chance of profiting from its marketing endeavours.

Notes

1 Kraus, E (2016) Consumer, B2B buyer shopping behaviors and how today's marketers are reaching them, *Marketing Desks*, [online] marketingdesks.com/b2b-buyer-vs-consumer-shopping-behavior (archived at https://perma.cc/M4XC-LGLN) [accessed 09 January 2019]

2 Domino's (nd) 'Create your own Pizza Legend [online] www. pizzalegends.co.uk/ (archived at https://perma.cc/6EY6-YHLD) [accessed 09 January 2019]

3 Dove (nd) Self-esteem project [online] www.dove.com/uk/dove-self-esteem-project.html (archived at https://perma.cc/W9NX-ZR38) [accessed 09 January 2019]

4 General Electric (2018) What's the matter with Owen BBDO New York [online] www.youtube.com/watch?v=wJZHXfcNZBU (archived at https://perma.cc/Q7QV-XWB8) [accessed 09 January 2019]

5 Matsa, K E and Shearer, E (2018) News use across social media platforms 2018: most Americans continue to get news on social media, even though many have concerns about its accuracy, *Pew Research Center*, 10 September [online] www.journalism.org/2018/09/10/news-use-across-social-media-platforms-2018/ (archived at https://perma.cc/UZ5S-PJ35) [accessed 16 January 2019]

6 Bergström, A and Jervelycke Belfrage, M (2018) News in social media, incidental consumption and the role of opinion leaders, *Digital Journalism*, 12 January [online] www.tandfonline.com/doi/full/10.1080/21670811.2018.1423625 (archived at https://perma.cc/X3B8-FWFU) [accessed 09 January 2019]

7 Jones, L, Milkman, K L and Berger, J (2015) The secret to online success: what makes content go viral - the psychological dimensions of what gets shared and shared and shared again, *Scientific American*, 14 April [online] www.scientificamerican.com/article/the-secret-to-online-success-what-makes-content-go-viral/ (archived at https://perma.cc/8T29-X3FV) [Last accessed 16 January 2019]

8 Neely, P (2014) 7 ways to get people to share your content, *Practical Ecommerce*, 05 August [online] https://www.practicalecommerce.com/7-ways-to-get-people-to-share-your-content (archived at https://perma.cc/3CVD-6ZK9) [accessed 15 August 2019]

9 Michelin Guide (nd) History of the MICHELIN guide [online] https://guide.michelin.com/th/en/about-michelin-bkk (archived at https://perma.cc/B2KD-JH4F) [accessed 16 January 2019]

WE ARE OPERATING IN A SERVICE ECONOMY

The Agricultural Revolution, in the 18th century, generated an increase in the production of food. It pushed out small-scale farmers and workers who were no longer required [1], and as a result, there were fewer opportunities to earn income in the sector.

These farmers ended up migrating to the cities, where they found work doing the new jobs created during the Industrial Revolution. They earned more money because they were adding greater perceived value than when undertaking the traditional farming work in which they were previously engaged. Thus, society became richer. Over time, the world moved from an agrarian to a product economy where more people were employed in the making of products than in farming.

This pattern has been repeated as manufacturing has become more efficient. The increase in productivity has resulted in fewer individuals being required in the making of goods. Over time, people have been employed in delivering services, adding greater perceived value and earning higher wages. Society has become richer, which has, in turn, fuelled the demand for even more services.

Both the move to products and then the transition to a service economy affected the public's expectations, perception of financial worth and priorities. People expected a greater level of customer service and more money was spent on services. Activities such as going out to eat became more usual occurrences, as seen in the growth of the fast-food industry in 1950s and 1960s America [2].

The commoditization of goods brought about the 'servitization' of manufacturing [3]. That is, manufacturers sought to create value-added services around their product offering in order to create competitive advantage, build revenue streams and improve profitability.

Today, globally we are a service economy. Services now account for 68.9 per cent of total world GDP. In high-income countries, services, on average, account for 74 per cent of GDP, and even in low- and middle-income countries, they now represent 57 per cent [4].

Until recently, productivity in the delivery of services was less efficient than in manufacturing. While in industry machines replaced people and made assembly lines more cost-effective, human beings were still required to provide many of the services that we purchased. This paradigm has been changed by the digital and technological revolution.

Tablets and mobile technology have made the ordering process more efficient in restaurants, resulting in fewer waiting staff being required. The Internet of Things spawning smart meters, boilers etc, means that the servicing and reading of domestic appliances can be undertaken remotely and requires less manpower. Call centre staff are being replaced by chatbots, and as the capabilities of artificial intelligence and smart assistants improve, it is easy to see how human beings will not be required in many customer service interactions. As an increasing amount of commerce goes online, the jobs that were available in retail are becoming scarcer. Driverless vehicles will most likely result in truck, bus and taxi drivers no longer being employed.

Just as the greater capabilities in the production of goods spawned the growth in services, we are now witnessing the same developments happening within the service sector itself. Human labour is being replaced by machines, and efficiencies in delivery are rendering services a commodity. Whereas the provision of specific service deliverables was a way of a business creating competitive advantage, increasingly they are becoming an expectation.

Services are now less likely to be a value add, and in all probability are provided in order to enable a company to compete. This situation means enterprises that still regard themselves as operating in the service economy will struggle to create a compelling proposition, and risk being indistinguishable from the rest of the market.

As services become commoditized, companies need to understand how they can add value in order to attract customers. The answer was provided by B Joseph Pine II and James H Gilmore in their seminal 1998 article 'Welcome to the Experience Economy' [5]. We are moving from an economy which was once predicated on the making of goods, and is currently dominated by the delivery of services, to one that will be based on the staging of experiences.

A good example of this progression is the motor car. Ownership of a vehicle was once the most cost-effective way of making use of this system of transport; cars were promoted as a product to be purchased. Technology gave rise to services such as Uber, which launched in 2010 and uses digital communications to connect passengers with independent drivers. Satellite navigation means that private individuals can now transport people efficiently and without specialist expertise, in contrast for example with London's black-taxi drivers, who are required to study 'The Knowledge' [6].

These developments have meant that for a significant number of city dwellers, car ownership is no longer cost-effective. For example, the average UberX ride in the United States is costed at $1.50 per mile; in New York City, car ownership works out at $3.00 per mile [7]. For many individuals, companies like Uber have made the car a service and not a product. Driverless cars will bring the price down further, which will result in car ownership being undesirable for the majority of people. Vehicles will eventually not be perceived as a product by the general public but will end up as purely a service offering. As the market matures, driverless cars are most likely to become commoditized, with price being the most obvious differential.

Technology and regulation will result in all these cars being capable of delivering passengers safely to their destinations. Every company will be using the same infrastructure – road system, GPS satellites etc. No longer able to compete on service, they will have to contend on the experience they provide, for example the luxury of the car's interior, the refreshments that are offered on the journey, the in-car entertainment – films, music, games on offer, etc. Loyalty to a particular company may result in greater levels of personalization, rewards, surprises and other perks. While every enterprise will be able to deliver a similar level of service, it will be the particular experience, designed for a specific audience, that may mean an individual chooses one supplier over another.

There are two fundamental differences between services and experiences. Firstly, as Pine and Gilmore explain, while products are tangible and services are intangible, experiences are memorable [5]. In other words, when putting together an experience, goods and services are utilized in such a way that creates an event, which is notable and easily remembered. Pine and Gilmore reveal that while products are made and services are delivered, experiences are staged [5].

A service can work effectively by simply being functionally efficient. For example, budget airlines can often provide a reliable and competent service without leaving passengers delighted and looking forward to flying with that particular carrier again. In contrast, experiences go beyond mere utility. The providers of an experience have to define how they want a customer to feel. The emotional deliverable is a key way for the creators of an experience to define its parameters. They then 'stage' the different aspects of the encounter to ensure that their client leaves having felt part of a memorable occurrence.

For example, a visit to an Apple store does not have to be merely about making a purchase. It uses its products and customer service to stage an experience in each and every one of its retail outlets. The products are laid out so customers can interact with them and learn about the different offerings available. The Genius Bar provides tech support but rather than simply being functional, it is designed like a concierge service at a hotel [8].

A purchaser of an Apple product will find the opening of the box an experience in its own right. In Adam Lashinsky's book, *Inside Apple*, he writes about how Apple had a dedicated room just to come up with the box for a product [9]. In other words, the experience goes way beyond the products themselves. Even opening the packaging has to engender the right feelings and emotions and appear significant.

Secondly, while goods and services are 'produced for' or 'delivered to' the customer, experiences are undertaken 'with' the purchaser. In essence, while most products and services are external to the buyer, experiences involve them – that is, they are engaged emotionally, physically or intellectually.

So, for example, many live events such as a concert or sports event are an experience because they are not external to the attendee. The sense of occasion is not just delivered by the musician, or athletes and teams, but also by the thousands of people who are also present. A big sports match played with no crowd would simply not be the same. Having a large audience is a necessary part of creating the occasion. The supporters, or fans, are not separate from the happening but a significant contributor to its success.

While plenty of TV shows and films do not deliver an experience, a programme or movie that moves a person emotionally, or stimulates them intellectually, will create an experience for the viewer. Similarly, while there are many restaurants that simply deliver a functional service for patrons, there are places that provide more of an experience. For example, the Jekyll and Hyde restaurant and bar in New York stages a themed experience for its guests. By employing a cast of characters and using special effects, patrons are transported back in time to feel that they are eating in a haunted explorers' club in the 1930s.

In the business-to-business environment, WeWork is an example of a company that goes beyond simply providing office space to rent. With its purpose to 'create a world where people work to make a life, not just a living', WeWork constructs office spaces that generate the building of communities and provide a sense of belonging [10]. In this way, the company goes from being a mere service provider to creating a whole interactive work experience for many of its users.

Motivated by not wanting people to feel out of their depth when it came to malfunctioning technology, Robert Stephens created Geek Squad, a computer repair service. The idea was to bring enjoyment and humility to the industry and not be intimidating, which tech experts can often be. Turning up in the black-and-white 'Geek Mobile' with a circular orange, black and white Geek Squad sign, and wearing the Geek Squad uniform of short-sleeved white shirt, black trousers and black clip-on tie, Geek Squad didn't just fix computers, it created a whole experience around the service.

We see evidence of an experience economy growing all the time. In retail, Nike Town stores are arranged as a concept town where buildings housing a specific sport surround a central square. Each week there are visiting athletes and special events taking place in the outlets.

The Capital One Café is a bank where people can grab a cup of coffee and a snack, do some work, use the Wi-Fi and, of course, talk to a money advisor. These open spaces are not merely functional buildings where banking activities can take place; they are there to enable people to feel comfortable, develop relationships, give value and provide more of an experience around any services that a customer may use.

As well as providing accommodation, Airbnb offers experiences through local 'hosts'. From sightseeing tours to workshops and classes, there is a plethora of interesting happenings on offer.

While technology is commoditizing service, social media is also fuelling the demand for experiences. Today, our online posts play a significant part in developing our personas and telling the world who we are. While sharing a picture of a purchase might be depicted as showing off and crass, taking a photograph at an event, at the top of a landmark or undertaking an activity is more relatable and accepted. Rather than boasting, it is perceived as providing a window into a person's life and what they are currently doing. Increasingly, there is more utility in what you do than what you own.

Leaving the agrarian economy behind did not prevent us buying food. In a service economy we still purchase a multitude of products. Of course, customer service will always be important, and companies will have to provide it in order to be able to win business. As we have seen the economy shift before, organizations need to understand it is happening again. Failing to comprehend that the world is starting to move on from the service economy will limit an enterprise's thinking, make it less likely they will be able to compete and prevent them from attracting the customers that they almost definitely want to obtain.

Notes

1 Study.com (nd) The Agricultural Revolution: timeline, causes, inventions & effects [online] study.com/academy/lesson/the-agricultural-revolution-timeline-causes-inventions-effects.html (archived at https://perma.cc/GWG3-RUHN) [accessed 01 February 2019]

2 Mealey, L (2018) History of American restaurants in the 20th century, *The Balance Small Business*, 21 January [online] www.thebalancesmb.com/history-of-restaurants-part-3-2888657 (archived at https://perma.cc/BX34-A69A) [accessed 01 February 2019]

3 Emerald Publishing (nd) What is servitization of manufacturing? A quick introduction [online] www.emeraldgrouppublishing. com/realworldresearch/strategy_growth/what-is-servitization-of-manufacturing.htm (archived at https://perma.cc/ZNL9-MMGU) [accessed 01 January 2019]

4 Buckley, Dr P, Majumdar, Dr R (2018) The services powerhouse: increasingly vital to world economic growth – issues by the numbers, *Deloitte Insights*, July [online] www2.deloitte.com/insights/us/en/ economy/issues-by-the-numbers/trade-in-services-economy-growth. html (archived at https://perma.cc/7A36-X4NS) [accessed 01 February 2019]

5 Pine II, B J and Gilmore, J H (1998) Welcome to the experience economy, *Harvard Business Review*, July [online] hbr.org/1998/07/ welcome-to-the-experience-economy (archived at https://perma. cc/3B3R-P5FZ) [accessed 03 February 2019]

6 Transport For London (nd) Learn the Knowledge of London [online] tfl.gov.uk/info-for/taxis-and-private-hire/licensing/learn-the-knowledge-of-london (archived at https://perma.cc/ZMH3-QHG3) [accessed 03 February 2019]

7 Harris, J (2017) Owning a car will soon be a thing of the past, *Guardian*, 23 October [online] www.theguardian.com/ commentisfree/2017/oct/23/owning-car-thing-of-the-past-cities-utopian-vision (archived at https://perma.cc/L634-6ZG7) [accessed [03 February 2019]

8 Swanson, A (2015) How the Apple store took over the world, *Washington Post*, 21 July [online] www.washingtonpost.com/news/ wonk/wp/2015/07/21/the-unlikely-success-story-of-the-apple-retail-store/?noredirect=on&utm_term=.f3b75d3892fc (archived at https://perma.cc/98G4-3HF6) [accessed 03 February 2019]

9 Lanxon, N (2012) Book review: 'Inside Apple' by Adam Lashinsky, *Wired*, 08 February [online] www.wired.co.uk/article/inside-apple-book-review (archived at https://perma.cc/57Y8-6ZNS) [accessed 03 February 2019]

10 WeWork (nd) Our Mission [online] www.wework.com/mission (archived at https://perma.cc/T68Y-SSD8) [accessed 03 February 2019]

THE CUSTOMER BUYING JOURNEY IS NO LONGER A LINEAR PROCESS

During a purchase journey people will make use of a number of resources including visiting websites, reading articles and blogs, reviewing frequently asked questions, downloading whitepapers and industry reports, looking at social media posts and conducting conversations on these platforms, watching videos, webinars and demos and referring to infographics, tip sheets, checklists, data charts, peer reviews and case studies.

As well as utilizing this online information, many individuals will also have internal debates and conversations with colleagues, conduct discussions with industry experts and personal contacts in their network, and interact with salespeople from possible suppliers.

With access to an array of information 24/7, buyers will go back and forth between the different platforms and channels available. From the outside, these activities might seem quite disparate. It may not be obvious how a prospect is processing and utilizing this information. These seemingly contrasting activities lead people to conclude that the path to purchase itself no longer happens in a sequential way.

This view, that the customer buying journey is no longer a linear process, has become increasingly popular in recent times [1]. This is not actually the case. What is happening is that people are getting confused between two different phenomena.

Before the World Wide Web, it was extremely difficult for buyers to go through a purchase journey alone. With limited access to information, an individual would have to engage with a representative from a possible supplier in order to ascertain the choices that were available to them.

In the consumer world this meant buyers would engage with estate agents in order to acquire a property or interact with the salespeople at a car showroom as part of the process of buying a vehicle.

In a business-to-business environment a buyer would flag themselves as a potential customer very early in the purchase journey. This is because, with little access to information, a person would have to engage with someone from a company in order to understand pricing, terms and conditions and other details of an offering. A buyer who didn't want to have this conversation could initially telephone an organization and ask for a brochure or further information to be sent to them. However, any savvy salesperson would follow up that request a few days later, to check the literature had been received and to try to secure a further meeting.

In reality this meant that salespeople would guide prospects through the purchase journey and could, therefore, ascertain where they were in the buying cycle at any given time. Of course, there may well have been more than one enterprise trying to secure the business and individual salespeople may have missed out to a competitor. Nevertheless, they would understand the path to purchase, as they were guiding the prospect through.

Today, this is no longer the case. Ninety-four per cent of B2B buyers report that they conduct some form of online research before purchasing [2]. The vast majority of these customers state that they conduct over half their research for a purchase online [3].

Whereas in previous times salespeople would be able to guide prospects through the purchase journey, buyers are now much more in control. There has been a shift of emphasis. Rather than salespeople determining the 'selling process', buyers are now in command of the 'buying process'.

Consequently, it has become difficult for enterprises to track their customers' buying journey. Salespeople are no longer able to guide prospects through the whole purchase cycle and in so doing ascertain exactly where they are in that process. Buyers are oscillating between visits to websites, conversations with experts, posts on social media, discussions with salespeople, reading articles, watching videos and utilizing case studies and peer reviews.

This lack of understanding as to where a buyer is within a purchase journey, combined with the seemingly random way a prospect will access the rich array of information available, has led people to claim that the buying journey is no longer a linear process. This is blatantly untrue.

While the way buyers conduct purchase journeys has changed, psychologically, human beings are the same as they always were. The cognitive steps in a buying process have not altered. There are a number of different portrayals of the buying journey but taking a model based on the work of US philosopher and psychologist John Dewey [4], the five steps are:

1 *Problem recognition.* The first stage of the purchase is the perception that a requirement exists. This can be stimulated internally – for example, someone feels thirsty. Alternatively, it can be instigated externally by advertising or word of mouth. It can also be created by the behaviour of others, for example everyone is buying an ice cream, has a new phone, etc.

2 *Information search.* A person will then look for a solution. This can be internal, relying on memory and experience. For example, if a person is thirsty, they may access previous memories of when a cold Coca-Cola or beer satisfied this requirement.

Alternatively, for a more complex purchase, they may start to explore possible solutions.

3 *Evaluation.* At this stage, a person will assess all the options they are aware of and select a preference based on a variety of factors. For example, the thirsty individual may decide a Coca-Cola is preferable to a beer as they have work to get done and a beer may adversely affect their performance. If they are in a store that has run out of Coca-Cola but has lemonade, they may decide that convenience and lack of time means that lemonade is currently the best solution. The complexity of the solution, the timescales involved, and the level of perceived risk will determine how long someone may take in evaluating a decision. If they cannot find a solution that is acceptable, they may choose to go back a stage to the information search.

4 *Purchase.* The actual purchase then takes place whether this involves paying immediately, placing an order or signing a contract. Of course, having recognized a problem, searched for information and evaluated the options available, a person may decide to do nothing. Often an organization doesn't lose out to a competitor, but the prospect simply decides to put the decision off or not proceed at all.

5 *Post-purchase.* The experience a company delivers, once a purchase takes place, will affect whether a customer tries to return the item or get out of the contract, buys again, is retained, leaves positive reviews or refers the supplier to others.

These sequential steps in the buying journey hold true regardless of the multitude of channels a buyer may access whilst making a purchasing choice. Claiming that the buying journey is no longer linear would be to suggest that the last few decades of technological development have psychologically changed the way human beings have made decisions for thousands of years. While consumers have a greater amount of information, in more places, than in previous generations, this does not alter the cognitive process with which decisions are made.

The speed with which a person goes through the various stages will depend on the acquisition. So, a special offer in a supermarket may lead to problem recognition, that is, the individual does not want to miss out. The pricing information will be in front of them on a product with which they are already familiar. They may evaluate, almost immediately, that it is a good offer and put the item in their shopping basket. The whole linear journey may take a matter of seconds on a low-risk and low-cost purchase.

On the other hand, investing in a high-cost business solution may take a long time. Having recognized a problem, a buying group may search for information. On evaluating the solutions available they may decide none are appropriate and go back a stage searching for more information. Another evaluation may lead to a proposal to make the purchase. On taking this proposal to the company's board, questions may be asked, which leads the buying group to re-evaluate and possibly even go back to searching for more information. While the process itself is linear, buyers may go up and down between the different steps before they are ready to make the purchase.

When salespeople were the main guides in a purchasing decision, it was relatively easy for an enterprise to make sense of the buying journey and ascertain where a prospect was in the buying process. With customers now taking control it is much more challenging for a company to know the buying stage the customer has reached.

While there are no definitive ways for an organization to know with absolute certainty where the prospect is in the process, there are indicators. As buying journeys migrate online, companies need to produce content which addresses different stages of the purchasing process.

At the problem recognition and information search stages, people are looking for possible solutions and appropriate options.

Therefore, an article, video or checklist that explores the different alternatives available to a buyer can be very useful. 'How to' videos and articles as well as short educational webinars or videos around the particular subject matter are all relevant material for this part of the buying process.

The evaluation stage of the purchase journey is where customers are trying to identify the most appropriate solution and best supplier for them. This is where webinars and videos that detail the solution in greater depth can be interesting. Case studies and testimonials, frequently asked questions, specification and data sheets and demos can all be valuable at this time. It is during this period that a company wants to illicit trust, ensure it feels like a safe option, demonstrate its expertise and be perceived as a supplier that can add real value.

While it is not an exact science, by understanding the particular content with which a prospect is engaging, a company will get an indication of where they currently are in the purchase journey. This may alter the way in which a salesperson approaches a prospect and the information with which they lead in an online message, email or phone call.

There is no doubt that purchase journeys have become more complex as buyers have greater access to more information in an increasing number of places. At the same time customers are undertaking more of the research and evaluation autonomously with less direct involvement and guidance from possible suppliers. Consequently, it is much harder for enterprises to understand the stage that a prospect has reached and how they arrived at a particular conclusion. This does not mean, however, that the buying journey is no longer linear. While the complexity may have increased, the cognitive process by which decisions are made has remained unaltered.

Notes

1 Whitler, K A (2018) If you think the customer journey is linear or a funnel, new research suggests you are wrong, *Forbes Media*, 08 September [online] www.forbes.com/sites/kimberlywhitler/2018/09/08/if-you-think-the-customer-journey-is-linear-or-a-funnel-new-research-suggests-you-are-wrong/#56c10e6d640a (archived at https://perma.cc/UY6N-6BR6) [accessed 04 March 2019]

2 Accenture Interactive (2014) 2014 State of B2B – procurement study: uncovering the shifting landscape in B2B commerce [online] www.accenture.com/t20150624T211502__w__/us-en/_acnmedia/Accenture/Conversion-Assets/DotCom/Documents/Global/PDF/Industries_15/Accenture-B2B-Procurement-Study.pdf (archived at https://perma.cc/2ZJ8-QXK6) [accessed 04 April 2019]

3 Forrester Research (2015) Myth busting 101: insights into the B2B buyer journey [online] go.forrester.com/blogs/15-05-25-myth_busting_101_insights_intothe_b2b_buyer_journey/ (archived at https://perma.cc/LS7A-XBGW) [accessed 04 April 2019]

4 Dewey, J (2011) *How We Think*, D C Heath & Co, Boston, New York, Chicago

I INSTINCTIVELY UNDERSTAND MY CUSTOMER

A new trend-conscious clothing brand whose target market is females between 18 and 30 years of age with mid-range incomes, is hiring a new marketing manager. One of the applicants is a 29-year-old woman who, on the surface, would appear to belong to the target market. Her last two roles have been marketing for a financial services company and, more recently, a technology business. The other applicant is a 52-year-old male. Although he is currently working with an olive oil producer, he has vast experience working with clothing multinationals. Who should the company hire?

Of course, on face value, the female candidate is most likely to have an innate understanding of the target market and be able to identify and empathize with the customer. That being the case, she would appear to be more appropriate for the role. On the other hand, admitting he has nothing in common with the customer will force the 52-year-old male to really study and learn about the market and understand the needs, challenges and aspirations of buyers. He has also worked in the sector before.

The truth is that with the information presented it is impossible to know which individual will do a better job. Success is not dependent on how similar the hire is to the marketplace they are targeting, or on their previous experience in the sector. It is all about how good they are at the discipline of marketing.

Either one of these candidates could fall into the trap of thinking they understand the market; the female because she is in the target demographic and therefore may wrongly assume her opinions represent those of the entire market; the man because he may rely on previous experience in the sector to inform the decisions he makes in the new role.

The fact is that most marketers are not a part of the target market with whom they are communicating. Even when they are, it would be a huge mistake to assume that they inherently understand the buyers. Merely working for the brand makes it impossible for a marketer to see its products or services through the prism of a customer.

First, the amount of time a buyer considers the average value proposition, or brand, is infinitesimal. Meanwhile, a marketing manager is thinking about targeting, the proposition, market positioning and communications every day. This alone makes it impossible to see the offering through the eyes of the prospect. An employee will also be influenced by internal conversations, personalities and company objectives of which a customer will have no knowledge and will not care about.

In addition, while a prospect will evaluate an offering based on their own needs, concerns, aims, aspirations and peer group etc, a marketer can't help their views and decisions being influenced by considerations such as their career progression, salary, bonus, personal pride and the opinions of, and their reputation with, colleagues.

There are too many individuals in organizations, from the CEO to senior marketing personnel, who, because they have a lot of industry experience, or consider themselves experts in marketing, assume that they innately understand their customer. It is this reasoning that leads businesses to create offerings that fail. It stems from making judgements that are inadvertently internally focused. It is the company equivalent of navel-gazing.

This approach is called 'product orientation'. Individuals will use their own hunches and opinions to focus on their organization, what they offer and what they do well. They will then create products and services based on these assumptions. Having developed the proposition, these enterprises will then go and look for customers who might buy from them. They will be under the illusion that their brand communications and salespeople, can enlighten the marketplace in order to persuade buyers to adopt the fantastic new offerings that the company itself has decided the market needs, based solely on the intuition and views of a few people.

This also happens with communications when companies produce messages that do not resonate with the market and consequently have little or no impact. Too often senior management or marketing departments have internal discussions about which logo, strapline, campaign idea, message or concept etc they prefer. They will vociferously argue for their point of view while highlighting their expertise due to industry experience or proficiency in marketing. All the while, this pretence that they inherently understand the customer, and consequently what is going to be effective in influencing the purchaser, proves only one thing: they actually know nothing about marketing.

The only way for any senior personnel or marketer to actually create offerings that are desired, and communications that are effective, is to be completely market oriented. Market orientation is the idea that any good business starts with the customer. A marketer's job is to understand the customer's needs, wants, desires, aspirations, challenges and the contexts in which these occur. Marketers are the link between the organization and the market. They can then use this information to create offerings and communications that resonate with those buyers.

The best marketers are not under the illusion that they are experts or that they innately understand their customer. Rather, they assume they know nothing, separate their own opinions and preferences from those of their customer and then go and find out.

This is undertaken by using both qualitative and quantitative research. Qualitative research comes from ethnography, that is, the study of people and cultures. In business terms it means getting out from behind the desk and going to speak with customers and prospects. It means frequenting the places where people buy and where they use the company's products and services. Ultimately, marketing is a contact sport. Without engaging with buyers and witnessing first-hand how they interact and utilize the offering, no marketer can be really effective and have a proper informed understanding.

Focus groups are also useful in this regard as long as they are made up of people who are truly representative of the market segment that is being targeted. Listening to their opinions, the way they think and their perception of the marketplace can be extremely informative.

For companies that have a really small target market, qualitative research may be enough to gain an informed understanding of buyers. Where enterprises have a relatively large target market, qualitative research then forms the basis for a quantitative study. Quantitative research is based on data that can be quantified – in other words, numbers, spreadsheets and analytics that can be collected. One of the most effective methods for quantitative research is customer surveys. The attributes about which you decide to ask in the survey should come from the qualitative research.

For example, the qualitative research might bring out that people perceive the company to be reliable, that the product is easy to use and that it looks great. It might also reveal negative attributes such as that prospects perceive the company's customer service to be poor. Using the simple Likert Scale, developed by American social scientist Rensis Likert [1], these different attributes can then be turned into questions. The scale uses a range of 1–5, from strongly disagree to strongly agree. So, to what extent do you agree that the company is reliable? etc. This attitudinal data will provide a reasonable understanding of how the market feels about an offering.

If these questions are asked together with behavioural questions regarding the brands people consider in any category and their preferences, usage and satisfaction, then a company can start to really understand what people think and to what extent these feelings influence purchasing decisions. The perceptions regarding one or two competitors mentioned by participants in the survey enables a business to comprehend how they are perceived in the market, the key purchasing criteria of buyers and what effect these different measures have on each other.

To ensure that the quantitative research undertaken is accurate, one must use the correct sample size. There are a number of online 'sample size calculators' which will come up in any search, and there are a few inputs required in order to work out the sample size. First, you will need to know the size of the market. Normally written as population, this is the number of people or businesses in the target market. For example, if the target market is lawyers in the United States, then there are approximately 1.3 million [2].

The confidence interval, or margin of error, represents the difference in accuracy between the answers given by a sample audience and the entire population. So, a confidence level of 3 would mean the margin of error is +/- 3 per cent. That means if 85 per cent of the people surveyed answered a question in a particular way, you would expect between 82 and 88 per cent of the entire population to answer in the same way.

Finally, the confidence level signifies how certain it is that the answers will fall within the margin of error. Most marketing surveys are performed at a level of 95 per cent. So, using a sample size calculator, if 1.3 million US lawyers are the target market, working on a confidence level of 95 per cent and a confidence interval or margin of error of 3 per cent, then a sample size of 1,067 lawyers would be required.

As well as undertaking qualitative and quantitative research there are some other useful tools that marketers can use to stay in touch with the market. Using a search engine such as Google to explore challenges, offerings and opinions can offer some insight. Researching on social media platforms and reading threads and conversations can also provide a certain amount of understanding about a marketplace. Reviews, blog comments, forums and Q&A platforms such as Quora can also contribute to gaining awareness.

Gleaning other data regarding areas such as volume of sales, numbers of users, market share of particular enterprises, demographic breakdowns, opinions and views of the market can also be obtained from organizations such as the Pew Research Center, Statista.com and YouGov.

Once decisions are being informed by a market-oriented approach, that is ensuring that there is a really good understanding of the needs, wants and aspirations of the market, there are a couple of other measures that will assist in assessing the impact of any marketing communications strategy other than, of course, enquiries, sales and revenue.

Brand tracking uses quantitative data to measure the target market's perceptions of the brand. By undertaking this exercise every year, a company can ensure that a brand is maintaining its relevance and reputation in the marketplace. It can highlight issues such as if people are starting to feel that a brand is out of date or is being surpassed by competitors. These opinions can often be spotted ahead of a drop in sales revenue, which enables a business to tackle the issues before it has a wider effect on the organization.

Finally, the Net Promoter Score, or NPS, is a simple and effective way of measuring the satisfaction levels of customers. Comparing the score with competitors, in the relevant markets, also provides some intelligence into how a company compares with alternative providers.

The strategic marketing decisions that companies make should not be based on people's hunches, previous experience or so-called expertise. In many ways, there are no marketing experts in as much as the dynamics of any marketplace are always changing, and customer requirements and expectations are constantly evolving. It is a fallacy that individuals have an instinct for what customers want or the next big idea that will be in demand.

Being market oriented doesn't mean you have to ask customers what they want. This will never lead to innovation as people don't know what is possible. For example, before the invention of the telephone, customers of the postal service would have asked for faster and more efficient mail, but not for a device that they could use to talk to people thousands of miles away in real time.

Steve Jobs was often quoted as not believing in market research because he stated that Apple's job was to figure out what customers are going to want before they do [3]. While this is true, Apple under Steve Jobs' tenure used focus groups and market research, as was revealed during its court case with Samsung [4].

This is because it is only by undertaking market research qualitatively and, when required, quantitatively, that both marketers and business leaders can ensure that they truly understand their customers. In so doing, they can create innovations and make informed decisions that are likely to be effective and produce the desired results for both customer and company alike.

Notes

1 The Editors of Encyclopaedia Britannica (nd) 'Rensis Likert – American social scientist [online] www.britannica.com/biography/ Rensis-Likert (archived at https://perma.cc/5U67-WB52) [accessed 01 May 2019]

2 Statista (2018) Number of lawyers in the United States from 2007 to 2018 (in millions) [online] www.statista.com/statistics/740222/ number-of-lawyers-us/ (archived at https://perma.cc/6NLP-FSLH) [accessed 01 May 2019]

3 Goodreads (nd) Steve Jobs > Quotes > Quotable Quote [online] www.
goodreads.com/quotes/988332-some-people-say-give-the-customers-
what-they-want-but (archived at https://perma.cc/H5TB-PPH7)
[accessed 01 May 2019]

4 Stern, J (2012) Apple v. Samsung: court documents include photos
of iPhone and iPad prototypes, *ABC News*, 27 July [online] www.
abcnews.go.com/Technology/apple-samsung-court-documents-reveal-
photos-iphone-ipad/story?id=16873818 (archived at https://perma.cc/
BN76-9WAD) [accessed 01 May 2019]

MARKETING CAN STILL RELY ON THE TRADITIONAL PURCHASE FUNNEL

Willie Sutton was a bank robber in 1930s and '40s America. He escaped from prison twice and was sent down for the final time in 1952 [1]. It has been estimated that he stole $2 million during his career, which would be around $20 million in today's money [2]. When asked by a reporter why he robbed banks, Willie Sutton is famously alleged to have replied, 'Because that's where the money is' [3].

Similarly, enterprises have always had to ensure that they are present in the places frequented by their customers and prospects because 'that's where the money is'. Before the world of digital communications, people did not have a lot of access to information. Without the means to easily research and assess the products, services and solutions available, consumers reacted to the advertising, messages and information they came across.

Consequently, companies made sure they got in front of customers via the post box utilizing direct mail, using the telephone to make cold calls, attending relevant conferences and exhibitions and in the appropriate media through newspapers, magazines, radio and television etc.

Figure 23.1 Traditional purchase funnel

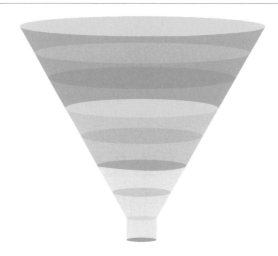

The model which was frequently used to understand the effectiveness of marcom activities was the traditional cone-shaped purchase funnel as pictured in Figure 23.1.

The reason for the wide top was due to the transient nature of the communications. For example, if a person was not currently in the market for a new kitchen, then it was likely that a direct mail piece containing special offers on kitchens would end up in the garbage. Similarly, an advert for kitchens in a magazine would be seen and quickly forgotten, while the periodical itself would either be thrown away or sit gathering dust on a shelf.

As only a small percentage of any marketplace is ready to buy at a particular time, even the most effective adverts would garner a relatively small amount of response. In this scenario the greater the number of relevant prospects a business could get in front of, the larger the number of enquiries it would receive. A wide top signified that an organization would try to reach as many relevant prospects as possible.

In the consumer world, individuals would screen themselves out of the process simply by ignoring the messages. The small part of the funnel at the base represented the comparatively few prospects whom any marketing activity would turn into customers, as compared with the number who were communicated with at the top.

In a business-to-business environment, prospects who responded to the communications would have to be followed up by individuals, either through written correspondence or by phone as well as face to face. Companies had no resource to concern themselves with the potential buyers who had not responded. With a finite amount of time, salespeople would concentrate their efforts on the people most likely to buy in order to achieve results and hit targets. This is why the purchase funnel became increasingly narrow, as prospects would drop out of the process leaving the few customer successes at the base.

The traditional purchase funnel was created by St Elias Elmo Lewis in 1898 [4]. It is hard to believe that a concept, developed well over 120 years ago, is still the ideal model for commerce today. As we shall see, the reality is that the traditional purchase funnel is a framework on which people should no longer rely. Instead, I would recommend that businesses use the Digital Sales Funnel shown in Figure 23.2.

The Digital Sales Funnel is so called because it reflects the changes that have taken place as a consequence of digital technology. However, the model can be used across all marketing channels.

There are a number of reasons why the traditional funnel is antiquated. Firstly, the funnel was created at a time when, in relative terms, attention was abundant. In 1898 people didn't experience the deluge of junk mail and circulars that are received today. It is safe to assume that back then, the mail put through a person's letterbox was read. While people have always used advertising breaks to make coffee, get a snack and go to the toilet etc, in the golden age of television, when there were only a few TV channels, the masses of people who watched the big family evening shows were a captive audience.

Figure 23.2   Digital sales funnel [5]

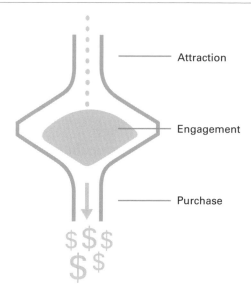

Today, in a world of information overload, multiple digital channels and an abundance of communications being pitched at us all
the time, attention has become one of the scarcest resources on the
planet. The model of simply purchasing attention in order to sell
products and services is unsustainable for many businesses.

This is combined with the fact that consumers are no longer reac-
tively using the communications they receive from companies to
begin looking for products or services. Increasingly, purchase journeys are starting online, with proactive consumers searching on the
web, social media, forums and review sites for possible suppliers [6].

Consequently, attention is no longer only sought via expensive
campaigns, as reflected by the wide top in the traditional purchase
funnel model. While there may be occasions when an organization
decides to pay to be noticed by a large audience, obtaining attention
is now an ongoing process. Company websites and social media
pages require constant content, and, unlike a newspaper advert or
TV commercial, can be seen and accessed at any time.

Cumulatively, a company may get in front of as many prospects as they ever did, but rather than doing this with a series of large campaigns, it is an ongoing process. The narrower top of the Digital Sales Funnel reflects the fact that organizations should be constantly garnering attention by continually creating valuable content for their online media.

While a direct mail promotion or radio commercial has a limited shelf life, and only works at the moment it is seen or heard, online media can be accessed at any moment and therefore has greater longevity. Tactics such as pay per click and retargeting tend to be used over a longer time frame than a traditional advertising campaign which may only run for a few weeks. These mechanisms work by providing a steady stream of enquiries rather than the one-off hit created with advertising. Even when a bigger marketing push is undertaken it shouldn't detract from the continuous activity demanded by online media.

The Digital Sales Funnel reflects the fact that while companies may still utilize traditional media and pay for attention, this is a boost to the other channels that are always on and didn't exist in a previous age. There is now a necessity to be constantly attracting prospects through the media channels an organization owns. The Digital Sales Funnel represents the reality that obtaining attention is a constant everyday activity rather than a task performed with a few sporadic campaigns throughout the year.

The middle of the traditional purchase funnel reflected the fact that while a company initially communicated with a large audience, this group would steadily decrease in size down to the relatively small number of people who would become customers. While loyalty schemes and memberships allowed constant communication with existing customers, there was no way, in the consumer world, for engaging with prospects other than the big expensive media campaigns.

In business, salespeople were responsible for nurturing leads and turning interested prospects into customers. As the mechanisms for undertaking this were all person-to-person communications, this was a time-consuming process. Salespeople were limited in the number of prospects they could handle at any one time. The consequence of all this was that companies paid to grab the attention of potential customers, but they had no mechanism to follow up those who didn't buy or respond and reveal themselves as being interested.

Now businesses own media channels. Just as with traditional TV, newspapers and magazines, digital media, such as websites and pages on social platforms, enable companies to build an audience and retain it through the content that they create. In order to achieve this, a company has to produce material that has a value beyond a purchase. In the business-to-business world this may be through organizations providing insights around industry trends, best practice and the latest news. In the consumer world it might be through celebrities, trends and fashion, lifestyle tips and competitions.

This content enables an organization to win attention and potentially keep it even when a prospect is not in the market to buy. Nurturing an audience was previously inordinately expensive. Sending out letters cost money for each one posted. Sales resource was used up with every individual conversation a salesperson undertook. Today, a certain amount of engagement and lead nurturing can be done en masse. The cost of producing a video is fixed, whether it is seen by 20 people or 20,000. Not only does owning media enable a business to build an audience, but in a world where attention is becoming increasingly scarce and therefore valuable, it makes commercial sense.

The traditional purchase funnel contains no mechanism to measure the building of an audience. The whole model is based on the fact that you start with a large audience which then becomes progressively smaller.

The Digital Sales Funnel reflects the new paradigm in the middle engagement section of the funnel. Once an enterprise obtains a prospect's attention, in an ideal world, it is an asset it never wants to lose. Why would an organization want to pay for that person's attention again when it can use the content it produces to engage, nurture and keep the attention it already has? The middle of the funnel becomes the biggest section because owning media channels provides an enterprise with the opportunity to cost-effectively engage a large number of potential buyers on an ongoing basis.

In fact, unlike the traditional purchase funnel, the Digital Sales Funnel enables a business to measure the amount of attention it has. This is important in a world where attention is becoming increasingly precious. For example, if a company's target market is 1 million potential customers and it has built an engaged audience of 200,000, it has 20 per cent of the potential market's attention.

Engaging with this audience of potential buyers on a frequent basis will mean that when a prospect is ready to make a purchase, the business that has built this audience will certainly be considered. Furthermore, the enterprise would have built credibility and trust with the prospect though this engagement. Assuming they have enjoyed some of the content produced, while not guaranteed, there is a good chance of winning the business.

Media works by building an audience and then ensuring it is retained. Every media company from Netflix to the BBC, the *Financial Times* to the *Washington Post* has the same aim. Companies today own media channels, which provide them with mechanisms to engage and nurture prospects on a scale that was previously impossible. The traditional purchase funnel provides no model and mechanism for reflecting this reality. This is why the Digital Sales Funnel is now required.

Notes

1 The Editors of Encyclopaedia Britannica (2019) Willie Sutton American Criminal [online] www.britannica.com/biography/Willie-Sutton (archived at https://perma.cc/JA49-R9B6) [accessed 03 May 2019]

2 Official Data Foundation (2019) 'U.S. Inflation Rate, $2,000,000 in 1952 to 2019 [online] www.in2013dollars.com/us/inflation/ 1952?amount=2000000 (archived at https://perma.cc/L7VM-XY5V) [accessed 03 May 2019]

3 Quote Investigator (nd) I rob banks because that's where the money is [online] quoteinvestigator.com/2013/02/10/where-money-is/ (archived at https://perma.cc/ZG9L-WCNU) [accessed 03 May 2019]

4 Hall, S (2013) How inbound marketing aligns with the new purchase loop [blog] *Hubspot*, 8 February [online] blog.hubspot.com/blog/ tabid/6307/bid/34158/How-Inbound-Marketing-Aligns-With-the-New-Purchase-Loop.aspx (archived at https://perma.cc/8WEB-FHB5) [accessed 03 May 2019]

5 Sticky Marketing Club (2016) Digital Sales Funnel [online] www. stickymarketing.com/downloads/ (archived at https://perma.cc/89VG-833K) [accessed 03 May 2019]

6 Forrester Consulting (2016) Why search + social = success for brands: the role of search and social in the customer life cycle [online] www.catalystdigital.com/wp-content/uploads/WhySearchPlusSocial EqualsSuccess-Catalyst.pdf (archived at https://perma.cc/M64S-XAR4) [accessed 03 May 2019]

CREATING CONTENT TAKES TOO MUCH TIME AND MONEY

Content marketing is not new. One of its earliest examples was in 1885 when the manufacturing company John Deere launched a magazine called *The Furrow*, presenting information to farmers. By providing expert advice, John Deere built trust and credibility with its audience [1].

In 1900, brothers André and Édouard Michelin, founders of the Michelin Tyre Company, published their first *Michelin Guide* book. They believed that by giving motorists information on where to find the best restaurants and accommodation, they would encourage car owners to drive more and consequently use their tyres [2].

What these two examples of content marketing have in common is that they both provided inherent value for their audience. The first documented use of the actual term 'content marketing' was by John Oppedahl in 1996 [3]. He was leading a roundtable discussion at the American Society for Newspaper Editors about using content to market newspapers more effectively, and audience value was a big part of that discussion.

Since that time, the World Wide Web has matured, and social platforms have become ubiquitous. As a consequence, the nature of content marketing has changed, although the requirement to provide value to the audience has not.

In previous generations, content marketing was a route to market in the same way as a business might decide to utilize direct mail, radio or TV advertising. Today, content marketing is no longer a mere tactic, rather it is an outcome of the world we now inhabit. In the digital age, every enterprise is a media organization because every company owns media channels. With digital media becoming an increasingly important part of the purchase journey [4], most companies do not have the option of opting out of owning this digital real estate.

A TV station is simply an infrastructure. It is a set of cables with a license to broadcast. What makes any television channel compelling is the content the owner chooses to transmit. Similarly, a website is dead space on the World Wide Web. A YouTube channel is dead space on the biggest video network in the world and a Facebook Page or Instagram account is dead space on two of the largest global social networks. Just like a TV channel, what makes any of these platforms compelling is the valuable content a business chooses to put on them.

Too many organizations leave their website, or social media platforms, static with no new content or information for weeks or even months at a time. They then wonder why these digital channels are not working for them.

Content is the currency of media. Without producing a constant stream of valuable material these digital channels will never be effective. The challenge is that many businesses think that creating enough content takes too much time and money and is, therefore, an impossible task. This is not the case. The key is to recognize that every enterprise today is a media business and to think like a media organization.

The first step in being able to produce a lot of content, with limited time and money, is planning. Here is an interesting exercise. Go and buy a daily newspaper and rip out everything that could have been written more than a few days ago. What you might find surprising is how little of the newspaper you have left. While the first few pages of news stories and the back pages of sports events obviously happened in the last 24 hours, so much else in the paper is prepared in advance.

There are often opinion pieces addressing trends that while current have been planned over a few weeks. Entertainment sections may cover a celebrity's visit to a city or a new film release which, while topical, was known about and created in advance. Sections such as Fashion, Living and Technology, while dealing with present issues, can all be arranged over weeks, or even months, rather than days. Similarly, while there may be times when a business wants to react instantly to an occurrence in the market, most material, while needing to be relevant, can be put together ahead of time.

In order to achieve this, I would advise any company to take a calendar wall planner and fill in all the year's significant dates. This can start with public and school holidays. Mark down big sporting events that are relevant such as the Super Bowl, Olympic Games or FIFA World Cup, as well as those smaller sporting events that might be important to the particular country, community or area that an enterprise serves.

Any big cultural happenings relating to a particular country or area such as the Glastonbury Festival in England, the Rio carnival in Brazil or the Edinburgh Festival in Scotland, as well as more general occurrences such as the Oscars in the United States or the Eurovision Song Contest in Europe can be noted. Political events like a presidential or general election should be added. There may also be some significant meetings within a company's particular industry such as its big annual conference, awards dinner or exhibition.

Having a plan of the year is helpful for a number of reasons. First, it allows a business to identify when the more convenient times and less pertinent moments will be to release material. It may also present opportunities to develop some content around a particular occasion. For example, a business may decide to release some market research ahead of its industry conference where there is most chance of getting exposure and being talked about.

Second, the year plan can also assist in creating content that is interesting for an audience by using a technique called combined relevance [5]. The approach involves taking something that a company's audience may be interested in and combining it with the product, service or subject matter it wants to talk about.

For example, if a really popular TV show such as the *X Factor* is getting 10 million viewers at the weekend then, by probability, some of a company's customers are probably watching. So, if a business, let's say a communications consultancy, can take the *X Factor* and combine it with a topic it wants to bring to its audience's attention, it automatically becomes more interesting. A title such as 'What the X-Factor can teach you about marketing' is very likely to get people clicking. Events on the year planner might well lead to some of these opportunities for utilizing combined relevance.

Finally, once the wall chart is completed, a business can start to put together a content plan for the year. This is essential for being able to produce material with a minimum use of time, and in a cost-effective way, in that it enables an enterprise to generate content in bulk.

In producing a TV series, no film company would gather cast and crew together to make one episode of a show. Imagine shooting Monday through Thursday and then editing the show over Friday and Saturday for a Sunday viewing. In the meantime, suppose that the entire ensemble had gone home for the weekend no matter where in the world they resided. The following Monday everybody would have to return for episode two.

Of course, it would be inordinately expensive and inefficient to film in this way. Employing the entire cast and production team for weeks on end while they travelled in from all over the world would make no sense. The other challenge would be that if one of the lead actors took ill during the week, then suddenly Sunday would come along and there would be no episode to show. The broad-caster would have to announce to an expectant audience that it was showing an alternative programme as this week's episode was not made due to Jill being sick.

While this seems ridiculous, this is how many companies try to produce content. They will decide to put out a blog post every Monday and often try and write it close to, or even on, the day. Suddenly the demands of the business mean an individual is distracted and Wednesday comes and goes with still no blog being posted. The momentum is lost and before they know it, weeks have gone by with no fresh content on the website or social platforms.

Like all media companies, in order to be effective, an organization must bulk produce content. For example, rather than blog once a week, book half a day in the diary once a month and write three or four blogs in one go. In this way, the next few weeks are organized.

Video is vital. It accounted for 75 per cent of all web traffic in 2017 and it is estimated this will be 82 per cent by 2022 [6]. Many businesses perceive video to be too expensive to produce in any quantity, and of course it will be expensive if an organization hires a camera crew to make one or two videos – the key is to produce it in bulk.

A business can hire a hotel conference room for a day. It may organize four members of staff to make three two-minute vlogs each. This may take until lunchtime. During the afternoon four different guests, made up of industry and subject experts, interesting clients or influential third parties, can be invited to be interviewed. Subjects should be planned so each topic is a few questions and the interview only two to five minutes long. In this way, six short interviews can be filmed with each guest. For a day's filming a company could, therefore, come away with between 30 and 40 separate videos. Posting one a week would represent more than half a year's material for one day of filming.

Moreover, a business could then transcribe these videos and use a copywriter to turn each one into an article, which could then be read to become podcasts. Consequently, from one day of filming, an organization could have a really extensive amount of material. By utilizing the wall calendar, planning content well in advance and then producing it in volume, companies can create relevant content on a tight budget using a minimum of time. In a world where every organization owns media channels it is thinking like a media business that will make this possible.

Notes

1 White, R L (nd) The history of content marketing: an essential guide [blog] *Track Maven* [online] https://trackmaven.com/blog/history-of-content-marketing/ (archived at https://perma.cc/6A9D-7GG8) [accessed 06 May 2019]

2 Feloni, R (2014) How the Michelin Guide made a tire company the world's fine dining authority, *Business Insider*, 20 October [online] www.businessinsider.com/history-of-the-michelin-guide-2014-10?r=US&IR=T (archived at https://perma.cc/UW83-63WR) [accessed 06 May 2019]

3 WebFX (nd) The beginner's guide to content marketing – Chapter 2 – the history of content marketing [online] www.webfx.com/marketing-guides/content-marketing-guide/history-of-content-marketing.html (archived at https://perma.cc/TB9D-VJBE) [accessed 06 May 2019]

4 Forrester Consulting (2016) Why search + social = success for brands - the role of search and social in the customer life cycle [Online] www.catalystdigital.com/wp-content/uploads/WhySearchPlusSocialEqualsSuccess-Catalyst.pdf (archived at https://perma.cc/Q7LF-UKJ7) [accessed 03 May 2019]

5 Zarrella, D (2010) Zombie marketing: how to use combined relevance to go viral, 14 January [online] http://danzarrella.com/zombie-marketing-how-to-use-combined-relevance-to-go-viral/ (archived at https://perma.cc/363N-BC5B) [accessed 06 May 2019]

6 Cisco (2019) Cisco visual networking index: forecast and trends, 2017–2022, White Paper [online] www.cisco.com/c/en/us/solutions/collateral/service-provider/visual-networking-index-vni/white-paper-c11-741490.html (archived at https://perma.cc/Y28A-KDDE) [accessed 06 May 2019]

SOCIAL MEDIA IS NOTHING MORE THAN SOME ALTERNATIVE CHANNELS TO MARKET

When, in the 15th-century, Johannes Gutenberg designed the first printing press which mechanized the transfer of ink from moveable type to paper, he created a truly transformational technology [1]. Gutenberg's printing press started the process of democratizing information. Knowledge was no longer concentrated in the hands of the elite but could spread far and wide. Without print, neither the Reformation nor the Renaissance would have happened. In other words, Gutenberg's invention changed the world.

There have, of course, been other innovations since. While the significance of cinema, radio and television cannot be overstated, they were continuations of the developments initiated by print. These media enabled information to spread even faster and become yet more accessible. It could be argued that the World Wide Web finished what print started. We now have access to virtually all the information we require 24/7. This is hugely significant in itself, but the web is changing the world in a way that is characteristic of the impact that print had so many centuries ago.

While Gutenberg's printing press started the journey of democratizing knowledge, the World Wide Web has democratized its distribution. Although print, cinema, radio and television allowed information to spread further and faster than ever before, the dissemination of that content was controlled by media enterprises. Without the patronage of a publisher, film studio, record company or TV network etc, people could not get their voices heard.

The World Wide Web has enabled individuals and organizations to own their own distribution channels through entities such as a website or blog. For most people the easiest way to have their own media channel is through the social platforms that the web has given rise to, such as Facebook, Instagram, Twitter or LinkedIn.

These platforms have empowered the population. People's thoughts and ideas are no longer restricted to telling a few friends and colleagues. The masses now have a voice and want to use it. Today everyone, from individuals to small businesses, not-for-profit organizations to large corporations, can directly reach an audience through their own means of distribution. While this is a new paradigm for those who inhabited a world before the World Wide Web, there are now generations who have never known anything different and have grown up in a world where they have always had a voice.

There are too many companies that treat social media platforms as if they are simply alternative channels with which to reach the market. These businesses fail to see that social media is not merely a channel to market; it represents a cultural shift in the way people think and operate, and it is affecting almost all market sectors.

We used to discover music by listening to a DJ playing a new song on the radio, or by going into a record shop and flicking through the vinyl, cassettes or CDs. Streaming services mean that now, a lot of music discovery comes from sharing playlists with mates and following friends and celebrities to see what they are listening to and recommending. In other words, music has gone social. If this phenomenon was restricted to music then it would not be such a big change. After all, music, to an extent, has always been social. People have regularly gone around to their buddies' houses to listen to music, discuss bands and recommended albums. However, this is now happening in a multitude of markets.

Crowdfunding sites allow entrepreneurs to share their business ideas with the wider public. They can present their concept, and individuals can then contribute small amounts of money to get that business started. While music has always been social, the funding of businesses has not. Neither has getting a job; but through platforms such as LinkedIn, people now share CVs and post messages on networks in order to find work.

There is almost no market sector that has not been affected by this socialization of business. In retail, both Amazon and eBay provide individuals with huge distribution, where they can sell goods to a mass market. The ability to write reviews on these sites enables people to let others know what the product and seller were like.

In hospitality, Airbnb allows anyone to rent out a property or create a local experience for travellers to purchase. Both Airbnb and other sites such as Trip Advisor provide people with an outlet to let others know their opinions. In transport, apps such as Gett and Uber enable passengers to give drivers a rating that other commuters can use as a guide.

The list goes on and on. For example, in the world of philanthropy, sites such as Just Giving and Kiva enable people to support good causes, see others who are helping and leave comments of encouragement. Social is not just a platform that people interact with on their smart phone, it is cultural. It is a way of thinking.

This shift has a number of ramifications for marketing today. Firstly, Francis Bacon famously said, 'Knowledge is power' [2], but this is no longer the case. Before the World Wide Web, a company would have knowledge and a person would pay for access to this expertise. For example, a client may go to a law firm because the lawyers knew how to write contracts of employment and the client did not.

Today, knowledge is everywhere. If someone wants a contract of employment, they can go online and download many up-to-date templates. Simply having the knowledge is not enough for a company to obtain customers. In fact, in the digital age, by protecting that knowledge and only revealing it for a fee, a firm may never be found.

Now clients will be attracted to a law firm that supplies online templates and detailed instructions on the best way to make the downloaded contracts work for their business. This content will help in driving traffic to the law firm's site and make it more likely that it is found. In providing these downloads the law firm is demonstrating that it is knowledgeable. In this way it can elicit some credibility and trust with its prospects. There will always be people who will use the knowledge available to put the contracts together themselves. This is fine. There will, though, be many others who, after some investigation, would rather employ experts to undertake the work for them.

In other words, today people don't pay for knowledge, they pay for the application of that knowledge specific to their circumstances. Consequently, knowledge is no longer power; shared knowledge is power. It is by sharing knowledge that a company can demonstrate its expertise and attract prospects to its business.

The American merchant John Wanamaker famously said that 'the customer is king' [3], but social media, and the resulting socialization of business, means that today, the customer is no longer king – they are now your partner. In a world where consumers have a channel, business needs to get customers involved. People no longer want to just be spectators; they want to be participants.

Involvement can mean enabling buyers to leave reviews in order to share their experiences, or provide a rating system, such as Amazon's five stars, so customers can demonstrate their level of satisfaction. It can also include providing customers with an outlet to come up with ideas for a particular enterprise. My Starbucks Idea is the coffee company's way of enabling consumers to make suggestions for new products or improvements [4]. Lay's encouraged customers to 'co-create' with the company when it ran its 'Do Us a Flavour' campaign, asking for people to invent new flavours of crisps [5].

Whichever way it is conceived, companies must now interact with their prospects and consumers in a manner that was unfathomable before the age of digital communications. It does not matter whether an organization is business to business or business to consumer – the age of customer empowerment doesn't make distinctions. Organizations have to open up and become more transparent. They must be prepared to let a little control go and be willing to enter into more dialogue and conversations with the market. In other words, business itself has become more social.

This affects lead generation itself. A company's target prospects are no longer just new potential customers, they are also a channel to market. Before digital media there was a clear separation. An enterprise would have an audience that it wanted to reach, and it would then utilize channels such as TV, radio, magazines, newspapers, direct mail etc as routes to get to this audience. While recommendations and referrals might come from existing customers, this happened via word of mouth and consequently there was no scale.

With everyone owning their own media channel today, and social sharing being a major way information is disseminated, this has changed.

An organization that is creating content of value can now build a significant audience of both prospects and customers. This audience is very likely to share some of this content with family, friends and colleagues. Although when sharing a video, for example, a person may not explicitly state that their colleagues should consider using the company's products or services, it is nevertheless a tacit endorsement.

People tend to associate with others like them. Whether it is mums, CEOs, football lovers, recruiters or people working in financial services etc, individuals are likely to have a network of colleagues in any group with which they identify. When a company's existing audience of both prospects and customers share its content with their networks this is a really credible channel by which a business can reach new people. Consequently, a company's customers and prospects are now a significant channel to market in their own right.

Social proof, that is what other people say and do, is one of the biggest influencers on human behaviour. The sharing of content with a person's network is one form of social proof but this leveraging of people's networks has another important ramification.

Before the age of digital communications, social proof was not easy to access. We could see some of the products and services that our friends used. Of course, people would ask each other for opinions and recommendations, but now, with the ubiquity of online communications and social media in particular, an increasing number of decisions are being made with a view to what people's networks and friends think. This is because, with social platforms and mobile technology, it is becoming easier to provide, and access, opinions about a whole array of subjects. In a world where we are faced with so much choice, using social proof to filter our choices and make decisions makes sense.

This being the case, companies need to encourage their customers to be involved, 'like' and 'mention' them in a positive light in order to garner as much social proof as possible. Power has shifted. Consumers now have outlets and channels on which to comment about the experience a company provides. Businesses need to encourage customers to leave as many positive comments and reviews as possible.

What used to be most important for companies was the image they conveyed. Millions of dollars would be spent by businesses to try to create irresistible sales messages. Consumers had little right of reply. Now, through the World Wide Web and social media, customers have an outlet and are literally producing millions of messages about organizations every day. It is not only what an organization says about itself that matters, today it is just as critical what others say. Brand is no longer just about the image an enterprise creates; it also relates to the reputation that a company earns. While this was always the case, it is the scale and transparent way that customers can share opinions with their own media channels that changes this paradigm.

Social media does not just present a business with some alternative channels to market. In the same way that the printing press precipitated fundamental societal changes, social media, spawned by the World Wide Web, is doing the same. Companies have to understand the cultural changes that democratizing the distribution of information has brought about, and how these have altered customer expectations. Social media is not just a set of platforms. 'Social' is a way of thinking and a state of mind.

Notes

1 Palermo, E (2014) Who invented the printing press? 25 February [online] www.livescience.com/43639-who-invented-the-printing-press. html (archived at https://perma.cc/D8R5-U3LX) [accessed 05 May 2019]

2 Garcia, J M R (2001) Scientia Potestas Est: Knowledge is power: Francis Bacon to Michel Foucault [online] https://www.researchgate. net/publication/233717484_Scientia_Potestas_Est_-_Knowledge_ is_Power_Francis_Bacon_to_Michel_Foucault (archived at https://perma.cc/AY2M-8XGG) [accessed 15 August 2019]

3 Salesforce (nd) Famous customer service quotes from famous business leaders in history [online] www.salesforce.com/hub/service/famous-customer-service-quotes/# (archived at https://perma.cc/H3PB-X8RH) [accessed 05 May 2019]

4 Starbucks (nd) What's your Starbuck's idea? [online] ideas.starbucks. com/ (archived at https://perma.cc/4GN2-UUDT) [accessed 05 May 2019]

5 Digital Training Academy (2014) Social case study: Lay's expands 'Do Us A Flavour' into year-long social media campaign [online] www.digitaltrainingacademy.com/casestudies/2014/01/social_case_study_lays_expands_do_us_a_flavour_into_yearlong_social_media_campaign.php (archived at https://perma.cc/3PMT-KY6X) [accessed 05 May 2019]

EVERY BUSINESS REQUIRES A 'HIGHER PURPOSE'

In his book *Capitalism and Freedom*, Milton Friedman stated:

> There is one and only one social responsibility of business – to use its resources and engage in activities designed to increase its profits so long as it stays within the rules of the game, which is to say, engages in open and free competition, without deception or fraud [1].

As Andrew Edgecliffe-Johnson pointed out in an article in the *Financial Times*, this doctrine of the primacy of shareholder value 'has defined Anglo-Saxon capitalism for almost 50 years' [2].

While the sole aim of a multitude of companies has been simply to make money and generate profits, there have always been enterprises with a 'higher purpose'. For example, in 1976, due to her concern about the environment, Anita Roddick started The Body Shop, creating cosmetics that were not tested on animals and which only used natural ingredients [3]. At the time, this was far from a mainstream approach to business. Although this was commerce with a conscience, Roddick's motives were not purely altruistic, as she also intended the business to be commercially successful and make money.

Similarly, when Bill Gates and Paul Allen started Microsoft in 1975, they believed in the positive impact technology could have on people's lives. Consequently, their vision for Microsoft was to 'put a computer on every desk and in every home' [4]. Of course, in so doing, Microsoft also became a phenomenal commercial success.

The idea of a company requiring a higher purpose has really become a more common part of business vernacular during the early part of this century. There are a number of reasons why this is the case.

The move to a post-industrial society where, in the Western world and increasingly beyond, people's basic needs are met, has resulted in more questions being asked about the purchases we make. Concerns about issues such as sustainability, the environment and social inequality are now at the forefront of people's minds. The rise of technology and challenges concerning areas such as data and privacy, the use of artificial intelligence and automation has also led to society facing ethical challenges which raise consciousness about factors not previously considered [5].

The internet has led to more information and a greater transparency regarding the behaviour of individuals, enterprises and organizations. We hold individuals and entities to a greater level of accountability because we have been empowered to do so. Whether this is a cause or an effect, trust in governments, business and the media is in decline [6]. Of course, other factors have contributed to this deterioration such as the collapse of Enron and the financial crises of 2007–2008. This leads to a scepticism which can, in turn, further our desire to know more about the companies that we use.

Owning media channels such as a website, as well as pages on social platforms like Facebook, Instagram and YouTube, requires enterprises to produce content that will interest their audience. Widening the scope of what a company stands for enables a business to create material that has wider appeal than merely talking about its core products or services.

Finally, the ubiquity of choice has led to the commoditization of so many offerings. Many enterprises have seen purpose as a way of giving their brand relevance while obtaining competitive advantage both in the battle for customers as well as in attracting employees.

While a higher purpose can be defined as an aspirational reason for existing beyond making money, this is not necessarily in conflict with Milton Friedman. As highlighted above, today's business environment may mean that an enterprise might actually achieve more commercial success with a purpose than without.

There are indeed some excellent examples of where this may very well be the case. Innocent's quest to 'help people live well and die old' [7] is not just a purpose beyond making money, it goes to the very core of its value proposition. In fact, Innocent is so named because its products are made with 100 per cent pure fruit and veg.

Similarly, Dove's campaign for real beauty, which rallied against the airbrushed pictures of so-called 'perfect' women [8], not only reinvigorated the brand, but was also a mission that went to the heart of its communications, was portrayed in an authentic way, and was backed up with thought leadership and educational initiatives [9].

There is no doubt that when a business has a purpose in which it genuinely believes, and which relates directly to its offering, it can be a very effective mechanism in the brand being more meaningful, relevant, desired and subsequently profitable.

The problem is that rather than 'purpose' being seen as a useful mechanism, which when meeting the criteria above can enable a company to be successful, it is now regarded by many individuals as an absolute requirement for success. This is simply not the case.

I have worked with plenty of successful enterprises that, when I asked them for their higher purpose, beyond making money, didn't have an answer. If a higher purpose is an absolute requirement for success, then quite simply these companies should not have been servicing customers, employing staff and making money. Yet the fact is there are successful businesses without a purpose operating prosperously right now.

The idea of an enterprise requiring a higher purpose has a number of limitations. First, while, of course, a founder can start a company with a purpose in mind, small businesses do not require a purpose. There are millions of successful companies operating around the world where success is dependent on the owner or partners. These companies do not have a brand but rely on the leaders behind the organization. Success is driven by personal relationships, customer satisfaction and individual reputation.

Human beings have innate value. Consequently, these small businesses driven by personal relationships do not require a purpose beyond the humanity exhibited between client and customer. From accountants to lawyers, gardeners to electricians, car mechanics to plumbers there are literally an abundance of successful small companies for which a 'higher purpose' is completely unnecessary.

It is really when a company goes beyond personal relationships, and when brand becomes relevant, that an enterprise may find a purpose useful. In order to be an effective mechanism, it has to be genuine and linked to what the company actually does. The belief that a brand requires a purpose, no matter what the circumstances, has led to some ridiculous examples of companies adopting a purpose that was neither genuine nor relevant.

For example, when trying to convey a message of unity, peace and understanding, not a prerequisite for a provider of soft drinks, Pepsi had to withdraw adverts that used social protests as a backdrop to its message when it was accused of trivializing a serious issue [10]. Similarly, Starbucks faced a backlash when it encouraged its Baristas to write 'race together' on coffee cups in order to start a conversation about race relations within communities [11]. This campaign did not come across as authentic and neither was it perceived to relate in any way to the company's offering.

The idea of company purpose has been made more popular by Simon Sinek's 2009 TED talk [12], which was also a book, *Start with Why* [13]. Sinek makes the argument that people do not buy what you do, they buy why you do it. While I am sure there are circumstances when this is indeed the case, it is a sweeping statement which is blatantly false in the majority of circumstances.

For example, Amazon's mission is to be 'Earth's most customer-centric company, where customers can find and discover anything they might want to buy online, and endeavours to offer its customers the lowest possible prices' [14]. This, however, is not a purpose. It is exactly what Amazon strives to achieve and why people give it their custom. People don't buy from Amazon because of 'why they do it' but because of 'what they do'. Yet Amazon is one of the most successful companies in the world. If purpose is an absolute requirement, how could this be?

Even when a company has a purpose, it is not necessarily the reason people buy. For example, Lego's purpose is 'to inspire and develop the builders of tomorrow' [15]. Yet if you stopped customers by the Lego section in any toy store and asked them why they were buying Lego, I am sure many more people will tell you that their children love it, that they used to play with it or that it is a fun activity that gets their children away from a screen for a while. I doubt that many will reply that they want to 'inspire and develop their children to be the builders of tomorrow'.

Similarly, while Uber's declared mission is 'to ignite opportunity by setting the world in motion' [16], I am not convinced that any of its customers would cite that as the reason for using the app. The far more likely explanation is that it is a cheaper and more convenient option than many of the alternatives. In other words, people don't use Uber because of 'why they do it' but because of 'what they do'.

For the majority of businesses their success will be determined by the value proposition they offer to the customer, and whether it is worthwhile and solves their challenges, or fulfils their aspirations, in a way that is cost effective to the particular marketplace they are targeting. This will be influenced by the competitors and alternative options that the consumer has at their disposal, as well as the company's ability to deliver the proposition consistently and effectively. In other words, 'what they do'.

This is not to say that purpose cannot be central in delivering success to a particular enterprise. When it relates directly to a company's offering it can provide a brand with meaning, enable it to be more relevant and desired. This, in turn, can lead to profits. Even when consumers do not buy from an organization because of its purpose, it may still have value. It can enable a business to be more consistent in its communication and help attract and motivate employees. However, to suggest, as some do, that for a business to be successful today, it is required to have a purpose, goes against the evidence and, while fashionable, is blatantly incorrect.

Notes

1 Milton, F (1962) *Capitalism and Freedom,* University of Chicago Press, Chicago, IL

2 Edgecliffe-Johnson, A (2019) Beyond the bottom line: should business put purpose beyond profit? *Financial Times*, 04 January [online] www.ft.com/content/a84647f8-0d0b-11e9-a3aa-118c761d2745 (archived at https://perma.cc/7K7K-V24E) [accessed 19 June 2019]

3 Entrepreneur Europe (2008) Anita Roddick: cosmetics with a conscience [online] www.entrepreneur.com/article/197688 (archived at https://perma.cc/6ZAR-6HKA) [accessed 19 June 2019]

4 Statt, N (2015) Microsoft at 40: read Bill Gates' anniversary email to employees, *cnet*, 03 April [online] www.cnet.com/news/microsoft-at-40-read-bill-gates-anniversary-email-to-employees/ (archived at https://perma.cc/2SL8-NF99) [accessed 01 July 2019]

5 Encyclopedia Britannica (nd) Postindustrial society [online] www.britannica.com/topic/postindustrial-society (archived at https://perma.cc/W8V5-NTMP) [accessed 01 July 2019]

6 Harrington, M (2017) Survey: people's trust has declined in business, media, government and NGOs, *Harvard Business Review*, 16 January [online] hbr.org/2017/01/survey-peoples-trust-has-declined-in-business-media-government-and-ngos (archived at https://perma.cc/Z3WR-Y374) [accessed 01 July 2019]

7 Innocent (nd) hello, we're innocent [online] www.innocentdrinks. co.uk/us/our-story (archived at https://perma.cc/RZ7C-TDJP) [accessed 01 July 2019]

8 Dove (nd) The Dove real beauty pledge [online] www.dove.com/uk/ stories/about-dove/dove-real-beauty-pledge.html (archived at https://perma.cc/3C47-L38W) [accessed 01 July 2019]

9 Dove (nd) Our Mission [online] www.dove.com/uk/dove-self-esteem-project/our-mission.html (archived at https://perma.cc/X6WT-RJMS) [accessed 01 July 2019]

10 Bond, S (2017) 'Pepsi withdraws Kendall Jenner ad after social media backlash, *Financial Times*, 05 April [online] www.ft.com/ content/3c811b64-1a33-11e7-a266-12672483791a (archived at https://perma.cc/ZRN9-XM6W) [accessed 01 July 2019]

11 Taylor, K (2019) Howard Schultz reveals how he decided to launch Starbucks' 'embarrassing' and 'tone deaf' 'Race Together' campaign despite internal concerns, *Business Insider*, 29 January [online] www.businessinsider.com/howard-schultz-failed-race-together-campaign-2019-1?r=US&IR=T (archived at https://perma.cc/ F3GY-6V5Y) [accessed 01 July 2019]

12 TED (2009) Simon Sinek, 'How great leaders inspire action' [online video] www.ted.com/talks/simon_sinek_how_great_leaders_ inspire_action?language=en#t-322 (archived at https://perma. cc/5TB5-HD78) [accessed 01 July 2019]

13 Sinek, S (2009) *Start with Why*, Portfolio Penguin

14 Amazon jobs (nd) We pioneer [online] www.amazon.jobs/en/ working/working-amazon (archived at https://perma.cc/9NLX-UP4N) [accessed 01 July 2019]

15 Lego (nd) About the Lego Group [online] www.lego.com/en-gb/ aboutus (archived at https://perma.cc/YMH5-XSQA) [accessed 01 July 2019]

16 Uber (nd) Our Mission [online] investor.uber.com/home/default.aspx (archived at https://perma.cc/7PYV-9GRG) [accessed 01 July 2019]

INDEX

Note: Page numbers for figures are indicated in *italics*.